WOMEN UNDER ISIS RULE: FROM BRUTALITY TO RECRUITMENT

HEARING

BEFORE THE

COMMITTEE ON FOREIGN AFFAIRS HOUSE OF REPRESENTATIVES

ONE HUNDRED FOURTEENTH CONGRESS

FIRST SESSION

JULY 29 2015

Serial No. 114–85

Printed for the use of the Committee on Foreign Affairs

Available via the World Wide Web: http://www.foreignaffairs.house.gov/ or http://www.gpo.gov/fdsys/

U.S. GOVERNMENT PUBLISHING OFFICE

95–695PDF   WASHINGTON : 2015

For sale by the Superintendent of Documents, U.S. Government Publishing Office
Internet: bookstore.gpo.gov   Phone: toll free (866) 512–1800; DC area (202) 512–1800
Fax: (202) 512–2104   Mail: Stop IDCC, Washington, DC 20402–0001

CONTENTS

WOMEN UNDER ISIS RULE: FROM BRUTALITY TO RECRUITMENT

WEDNESDAY, JULY 29, 2015

House of Representatives,
Committee on Foreign Affairs,
Washington, DC.

The committee met, pursuant to notice, at 10 o'clock a.m., in room 2172 Rayburn House Office Building, Hon. Edward Royce (chairman of the committee) presiding.

Chairman ROYCE. This hearing will come to order.

I am pleased to announce that this will be the first of several hearings on the status of women around the world. The committee has worked on a bipartisan basis to promote women in our development efforts through a number of bills that we passed out of this committee, and I believe these hearings will allow us to build on that good work.

Today, we look at the brutalization and oppression of women living under ISIS. This violence against women is almost without parallel, from widespread rape and trafficking to forced marriage and murder. Female captives, including thousands of Yazidi women and girls, are sold as slaves in modern day slave markets. One U.N. official described meeting with a woman in ISIS-occupied territory who was forced to marry 15 different men in 1 year. Some of these so-called ''marriages'' lasted only 3 days.

That is life under ISIS for these women today. As one witness will testify, much of this seemingly crazed and indiscriminate violence against women is in fact a sinister and quite calculated strategy that goes to the heart of ISIS's survival. By forcing local women to marry into ISIS, the group expands its demographic base while reducing the population of those diverse communities it seeks to eradicate and to replace.

Simply put, ISIS needs women—needs to control them—to establish its ''caliphate'' and give rise to the next generation of ISIS. That is why ISIS is investing heavily in recruiting foreign women to join its ranks. And with each girl who becomes brainwashed, ISIS has a new poster child for its jihadi girl-power propaganda.

Sometimes it can seem like all we do is look at the worst of humanity. So I appreciate the efforts of Mr. Watts, one of our witnesses with us today. I appreciate his efforts to elevate the voices of those courageous individuals who are working to counter ISIS, often at great personal risk.

For all the horrible atrocities being committed in this region, there are those incredible stories of strength and integrity, many of them from women and girls with the most to lose: From the Kurdish woman on the front lines against ISIS, who declares that she fights ''to take back the role of women in society.''

We appreciate the fact that so many of these Kurdish women, 30 percent of those battalions that you see, Kurdish battalions, are all-women battalions, fighting on the front lines. By the way, only with small arms and rifles, because they can't get access. We have not given them or sold them to the Kurds, the long-range artillery or mortars or anti-tank weapons that they say they need. But they stand and they fight as they say to protect all women in society and they protect others besides the Kurdish behind their lines.

And we have the female responders pulling victims from the rubble in Syria. These female units go out and take on that role. And we have the captured Yazidi girl described by Mr. Watts, who walked right past her would-be rescuers when she realized ISIS had staged an ambush for those rescuers, thus saving their lives at the expense of her own life.

These stories inspire us to act. Credible voices need to be heard. They need to hear the fact that ISIS land is not a utopia.

We must prioritize the physical and psychological welfare of those women and girls who have escaped from ISIS, many of whom have been subjected to unbelievable trauma, and we need to support leaders in the region who are confronting the stigma of sexual violence head on and calling on families to welcome back male and female survivors with open arms.

Although we focused today on ISIS, we know full well that Assad's brutality against Syrians includes not only barrel bombs and starvation, but also widespread sexual violence. Ranking Member Engel and I have pressed for the consideration of no-fly or safe zones in the region, and we are pleased to hear of Turkey's recently increased cooperation with the United States on this issue.

I had lunch with the Turkish Ambassador last week to discuss this issue. I think this is a very important step. I also just for a moment wanted to thank Mr. Engel for his long-time support over many years of trying to get a focus on what was likely to be the blowback in Syria as a consequence of the violence there, and also his efforts where he worked with me and others on this committee when ISIS first came out of the desert and called for air strikes.

We went a year without doing that, and we watched ISIS take city after city after city, across Syria and then across Iraq, and now have some 5 million souls under the control of ISIS. I think our air power should have been used back then in order to degrade and slow or defeat them when they were targets out on the open desert.

But I now turn to Ranking Member Engel, whose passionate leadership on the crisis in Iraq and Syria has been of great benefit I think. And thank you, Mr. Engel.

Mr. ENGEL. Thank you, Mr. Chairman. Thank you for convening this hearing and, as always, thank you for your leadership on this issue, and all the other issues that this committee confronts.

To our witnesses, welcome to the Foreign Affairs Committee. Thank you for your time, and I look forward to your testimony.

None of the issues that this committee deals with are simple, and the fight against ISIS is certainly no exception. Just this week we see two of our partners, Turkish and Kurdish fighters, battling each other. This situation is a mess, and there is no other way to put it. That doesn't mean we should look the other way. On the contrary, we need to dig deep, look at all of the aspects of this crisis, and keep working toward a viable strategy.

Today, we are addressing a particular concern of mine, the way women have been victimized in ISIS's brutal rampage. In ISIS-controlled areas, women have suffered horrendous violence, they have been separated from their families, and they have been bought, sold, and gifted as if they were property.

Nearly a year ago, ISIS began its deadly offensive on the Yazidi population in the Sinjar area of northern Iraq. As many as 50,000 Yazidis were forced to flee. Five thousand Yazidi men were massacred, and between 5,000 and 7,000 women and girls became ISIS slaves. We have heard the horrifying stories from survivors, accounts of systematic rape, torture, forced marriage, and other abuses. Girls as young as 12 have been raped, often multiple times and by different fighters.

Sexual violence has a long, dark history as a tool of war, yet it seems that this type of violence is central to ISIS ideology. ISIS terrorists are using rape in an effort to wipe away cultural diversity, religious minorities, and killing LGBT persons in order to realize their twisted vision of a homogeneous caliphate. Sounds a lot like the Nazis to me.

It is also troubling that more than 500 women from Western countries have chosen to join ISIS. Lured by online glorification of life in Daesh, women from the UK, France, Sweden, and other countries have been encouraged to abandon their communities and join ISIS. It really perplexes me. These women recruited to ISIS are then funneled into domestic roles, recruitment jobs, or all-women patrol brigades to enforce the group's perverted world view.

So today I am hoping our witnesses can shed more light on this problem and share their ideas on how to meet this challenge. What motivates the women who join the ranks of ISIS? What motivates anyone who joins the ranks of ISIS? An organization with such a brutal record of violence against women and girls, why would women want to join them? How do we disrupt these recruitment and radicalization efforts? And how can we assist women to be part of a solution?

We know that with the right tools and opportunities women can be tremendous agents of change in preventing violent extremism. How can we adapt our policies, integrating women to address some of the tactics ISIS uses to recruit and radicalize?

So I look forward to the testimony, to learning more about the specific challenges women face in confronting ISIS, and how we can best address the recruitment of women who join this heinous organization in Iraq and Syria.

And I want to add to what the chairman said. Three years ago, I put in a bill which would have authorized the aiding and equipping of the Free Syria Army. And I said this 3 years ago, and I say it now, I can't help but thinking if we had been there and had done it when it should have been done, might things have been different now in Syria? It is the Syrian people who are bearing the brunt of all of the atrocities that are happening, and I think the United States needs to be more than just a passive bystander.

So I thank all of our witnesses, and I look forward to your testimony.

Thank you.

Chairman ROYCE. Thank you, Mr. Engel.

We are joined this morning by Ms. Sasha Havlicek. She is co-founder and CEO at the Institute for Strategic Dialogue where she works closely on counter extremism. She also co-founded the Women and Extremism Initiative.

We have Mr. Edward Watts. He is the director and producer of the film Escaping ISIS, which features firsthand accounts of women and girls who escaped from the terror group. Mr. Watts has also produced other critically acclaimed documentaries.

We have Dr. Kathleen Kuehnast. She is director of the Gender and Peacebuilding Program at the U.S. Institute of Peace. Prior to this position, Dr. Kuehnast worked for 15 years in the international development field, including time with The World Bank.

Dr. Ariel Ahram is associate professor of government and international affairs at Virginia Tech. He has written extensively on Syria and on Iraq and on ISIS.

Without objection, the witnesses' full prepared statements will be made part of the record. Members will have 5 calendar days to submit statements and questions and extraneous material for the record.

Ms. Havlicek, if you could summarize your remarks. You will have 5 minutes each, and then we will go to the questions.

STATEMENT OF MS. SASHA HAVLICEK, CHIEF EXECUTIVE OFFICER, INSTITUTE FOR STRATEGIC DIALOGUE

Ms. HAVLICEK. Thank you so much Mr. Chairman and distinguished members of the committee. I am very honored to have been invited here today and to be part of this extremely important discussion.

My testimony is looking at the part of this challenge that you have already raised but that has been I think largely overlooked despite the extraordinary, unprecedented numbers of women that are flocking to join ISIS, that are leaving in particular Western countries and migrating to ISIS territory.

Girls and women are—and I think this is difficult to comprehend—it feels counter intuitive—choosing of their own volition to join ISIS and subscribing, submitting voluntarily, to their ideology and to their rule. Women in extremist and terrorist organizations of course is not a new phenomenon, but the numbers here are indeed unprecedented. There are now thousands of women worldwide that have emigrated to ISIS territory, just from Western countries.

The numbers that official estimates have suggested are well over 550. That number is taken from estimates at the beginning of 2015 and will have grown substantially by now. It is important to know that these are not foreign fighters. We tend to hear the media categorize them that way.

For now, ISIS prohibits women from entering the battlefield, but that does not reflect the violent narratives that these women project in their social media lives—social media lives that we have been watching and analyzing over the last year, with a dataset, a unique dataset that has been tracking the developments of girls who have left Western countries and joined ISIS territory.

So they are, despite the fact of not being combatants, proving to be as much agents of the group and its ideology as men: As propagandists and recruiters—as we have heard, they are prolific online—in particular Western girls—as part of peer-to-peer, very sophisticated marketing and recruitment strategies, goading men into action—that is also important to note: For a 15-year-old girl to be able to say, ''I have made it out here on my own. Why haven't you?''—but also as inciters to violence. And they are, again, goading people who cannot make it out to the battlefield to do as much damage as they can at home.

They are also, as we have heard, enforcers of strict pre-modern Islamic codes, penal codes, as part of the Al-Khansa all-female moral police brigade. And of course, as mothers of the next generation of jihadists, a role that is held in high esteem for ISIS, but also other jihadi groups.

The violence of their online narratives is striking, and my written testimony is scattered with evidence of what they hope to be doing in the longer term. There is a wishful thinking there that they will be enabled to join the violence at some stage later.

I think it is important we understand that this is not a sideshow. This is very much a core part of ISIS's strategy, and it is a part of the evolving terrorist landscape. It is a core tactic of jihadist groups, well before in fact ISIS emerged on the scene as the predominant group. And as such, they should matter to us more than they have to date among security and intelligence circles.

Why are they important to ISIS? They are in part PR, in part troop morale, and in part, and most importantly perhaps, state-building strategy.

Why are these girls going? For a long time, in looking at the challenge of radicalization, Western authorities and governments I think have been viewing this problem primarily through an equalities and socioeconomic lens. That has not borne out in our minds to be true by the data. Women in our dataset in particular defy easy categorization on socioeconomic lines. I think that is the case across the board, female and male recruitment.

It is true that the grievances that are articulated in these women's accounts, not dissimilar to the male grievance narrative around identity, around the Muslim community globally being oppressed and there being no intervention to stop it happening, specifically, on the identity side of things, these women talk about the Western emancipation project as a ruse, as a means to sexualize women.

ISIS, absurdly, is seen as freeing women from that ''tyranny.'' And so this jihadi girl-power subculture has emerged. There is a meme that I have included in the testimony, which is a parody of a beauty industry set of advertisements. It is a woman fully covered, and it says, ''Covered girl, because you are worth it.'' And so rooted in Western culture, this propaganda is quite clearly coming out of it but rejecting it.

But what has been largely ignored—and I think to our detriment—is what I see as the pull factors. The pull factors are a combination of an ideology that has been seeded over three decades—a Wahhabi Salafist ideology that is essentially the intellectual foundations for the movements that we see in play today, including, but not only, ISIS.

And ''Brand Caliphate'' has done more for the diversification of recruitment around the world than anything else, including the recruitment of women. There has been a major spike in female recruitment, because ''Brand Caliphate'' is more than just about fighting. It is about building—building a utopian vision of a pure Islamic state.

And so we need to be looking at how ''Brand Caliphate'' is succeeding to reach around the world through a digital era hypercharging of the narratives, extremely successful propaganda recruitment machinery that has essentially gone unchallenged, a recruitment machinery that combines iconic memes, apps that have been developed, an extremely sophisticated, very evolved, decentralized communication strategy that would be the envy of many social media marketing companies and organizations at large.

What to do? Just very, very briefly. We cannot beat the radicalization problem, the conveyor belt challenge, through drones or border measures. We need a proportional soft power strategy, a machinery that can close the gap we have allowed to emerge between their propaganda recruitment machinery on the one hand and our response, which has not been professionalized to date.

The objective cannot simply be to reduce the number of recruits, female or otherwise. It must be to undermine the underlying ideology if we are going to have a long-term impact on this challenge. Credible counter narratives are absolutely key. In our minds, we need to be undermining, in the first place, ''Brand Caliphate.'' And those that can speak to the heresy, the inauthenticity, of that Brand are vital.

We of course have been working with the largest global network of former extremists, survivors of extremism. Those voices, as we know, are particularly credible and important. We need more women in this space. We need to be growing those networks, so that we can incorporate women. Women, female-focused counter narratives are to date entirely lacking in the counter extremism space.

And so just as a last point, we need counter narratives and we need to be getting ahead of the curve with inoculation strategies, tools for those at the front line, whether teachers or social workers that are seeing the first signs of young people being groomed or young people being approached by radicalizers. And so we need a compelling set of tools, some of which we have started to develop, to get ahead of that problem.

We need more female practitioners in the CVE space. This is vital, because we need to be addressing this from a gender perspective. And we need a human rights approach that is consistent and sustained. We need to be upholding female human rights around the world in ways that perhaps we have grown lazy about and relativist in our approaches.

They have a massive head start, massive resourcing. We need to now scale up what we know works. We do know that a number of things work. We have data to prove that in the experiments that my Institute has undertaken in the counter narrative space we can reach the individuals who are at risk very directly, and we can have an impact by engaging with them.

So we need to implement that competition strategy, so that we can drown out ISIS both on and offline.

[The prepared statement of Ms. Havlicek follows:]

July 28th, 2015

The Islamic State's War on Women and Girls

Prepared statement by

Sasha Havlicek

Founding CEO
Institute for Strategic Dialogue

Before the

Committee on Foreign Affairs

United States House of Representatives

<u>Verbal testimony to the Congress Committee on Foreign Affairs</u>

Mr. Chairman and distinguished members of the committee: thank you for inviting me to testify today. It is my honour and pleasure to be here for this important discussion.

My name is Sasha Havlicek, founding CEO of the Institute for Strategic Dialogue (ISD), a London based 'think and do tank' that has been working on extremism, across ideologies, since 2007. I am honoured to have been invited here today to give testimony about the growing spectre of female radicalisation and the unprecedented numbers of girls and women joining ISIS.

My testimony draws from the research my Institute is leading in this domain, including a unique dataset based on the social media accounts of Western women that have migrated to The Islamic State in Iraq and Syria (ISIS) territory[1]. It also draws on the understanding we have acquired of the radicalisation process through initiatives like the *Against Violent Extremism (AVE) Network*, the largest global network of former extremists in the world, which my Institute runs. I additionally draw on research we have done on the way in which terrorist organisations are using the internet and social media, and from our experience trialling pioneering interventions and counter-narrative initiatives on and offline to start to

---

[1] Saltman, E. and M. Smith (May 2015), *Till Martyrdom do us Part: ISIS and the Gender Phenomenon*, (Institute for Strategic Dialogue: London),
http://www.strategicdialogue.org/Till_Martyrdom_Do_Us_Part_Gender_and_the_ISIS_Phenomenon.pdf.

engage with 'at risk' youth and compete with the extremist propaganda machine. Finally, I draw from my experiences leading conflict resolution programmes in the Balkans where, in the aftermath of the Yugoslav wars, I witnessed the seeding of an extremist ideology, alien to the local Islamic culture and traditional religious practices; a phenomenon mirrored in so many parts of the world.

My testimony will attempt to address the following questions:

- What is the nature and extent of ISIS's female radicalisation and recruitment drive?
- Why and how are they succeeding in engaging women and girls in such high numbers, including from Western countries?
- What are the expectations of those that travel to join ISIS and the reality of life once they arrive?
- Does this phenomenon matter? Do these women pose a threat, and can we do anything to counter this rising trend?

1) A shifting terrorist landscape: Understanding women, not just as victims, but as perpetrators of extremism

There is nothing new about women in extremist and terrorist organisations. On the contrary, across ideologies and throughout history, women have played a range of active, sometimes leading, roles in extremist organisations, from ethno-nationalist and separatist movements like the PLO, the Red Army Fraction and the LTTE to far-right groups and those who advocate violence in the name of religion. As protagonists for their causes, they have taken on roles in logistics, fundraising and propaganda dissemination as well as violent combat.

However, there is a tendency within Western societies (as well as security agencies), to view women, particularly Muslim women, singularly as victims of fundamentalist ideology.

It is, of course, true that women are disproportionately affected by the consequences of radicalisation and terrorism, not least as victims of conflict. ISIS in particular has perpetrated abhorrent crimes against women, leveraging sexual violence as a tool for embedding the concept of inferiority and enforcing a rule of terror within their territory.

These atrocities of sexual violence, enslavement and the torture of women should in no way be discounted in their severity.

However, no matter how shocking and counter-intuitive, despite the brutally violent images associated with ISIS, there are girls and women choosing, of their own volition, to join ISIS. And they are doing so in unprecedented numbers, subscribing and submitting voluntarily to their ideology and to their rule. We must not be blind to this important development. This is a trend on the rapid rise, with serious consequences. Indeed hardly a week has passed over the last year without news of a woman participating in extremism or terrorism. From Denver to Vienna, so called 'Caliphettes' are running away from home on their own or in small groups to emigrate to ISIS territory.

The growing numbers of ISIS women are proving to be as much agents of that fundamentalist ideology as men – as propagandists, encouraging other women and shaming men into travelling to Syria; as inciters of violence, goading those who cannot get to the battleground to do as much damage as possible at home; as brutal, sometimes violent, enforcers of strict pre-modern Islamic penal codes (as in the case of the Al-Khansaa all-female moral police in Raqqa); and as the mothers of the next generation of Jihadists.

And while the numbers of female recruits to the so-called 'Caliphate' outweigh the numbers of women migrating to other theatres of foreign conflict[2], women have been a focus within the jihadist context far before the emergence of ISIS.

Indeed, the engagement of women by Jihadist groups has been a core tactic and the roles women play within these organisations reflects both the ideologies behind the terror and the long-term goals of a group. Abu Musab al-Zarqawi, leader of Jama'at al-Tawhid wal-Jihad, which later evolved into al-Qaeda in Iraq (AQI), is arguably the ideological forefather of what we now know as ISIS. Al-Zarqawi had already begun the recruitment of women to the jihadist cause and used them both for logistics and suicide bombing missions. While ISIS does not currently use women as combatants, it has augmented its female recruitment drive internationally with unprecedented success.

It is estimated that thousands of women worldwide have willingly travelled to ISIS territory in support of the 'Caliphate' and, while this has been occurring for a period of over a year and a half, insufficient attention has been paid to the trend and to the significance of female involvement. This phenomenon must be taken into account seriously as a key part of a fast evolving terrorist landscape.

---

[2] It should be noted that there is very little data on the numbers of women traveling to other theatres of conflict, which poses a problem for comparative analysis.

2) Western female migrants to ISIS: Facts, figures and emerging trends

At the beginning of 2015, 4,000 foreign fighters from Western countries alone were estimated to have travelled to Syria and Iraq since the beginning of the Syrian conflict, and of these some 550 were thought to be women who had emigrated to ISIS territory[3]. That number is significantly higher now, though we don't have an accurate assessment. Estimates from countries in the region like Turkey, Saudi Arabia, Lebanon and Tunisia are well into the thousands though there is even less reliable, comprehensive data on the phenomenon in these contexts.

The Institute for Strategic Dialogue has for the last year been compiling the largest known database that tracks and monitors Western females who have willingly migrated to ISIS territory. Our female database is attached to the larger Male Foreign Terrorist Fighter database run by the International Centre for the Study of Radicalisation and Political (ICSR) out of Kings College London, allowing us to monitor relationship statuses, group dynamics and the effects of martyrdom on the female cohort.

Using open source data, our researchers have been tracking and archiving the social media accounts and blogs of these women across different social media platforms and then mapping their on- and offline networks and relationships[4]. In order to grow and retain this sample of females, our researchers use a 'snowball' technique, where female ISIS migrants are identified among the networks of other known ISIS members. The women have been designated as ISIS migrants if they self-identify as such and appear to reside in ISIS-controlled territory. The ISD-ICSR database has also grown using evidence from photographs, online interactions with other ISIS accounts and reports to help determine the probability that the person is geographically in Syria or Iraq. We have, moreover, interviewed former extremists who are now working as mentors to women convicted of extremist and/or terrorist related offences.

We refer to these ISIS women as migrants rather than foreign terrorist fighters because, at present, ISIS prohibits women from entering combat. The 119 women tracked in the database includes 13 separate nationalities across the West, with the majority originating

---

[3] Hoyle, C, A. Bradford and R. Frenett, (January 2015) *Becoming Mulan: Female Western Migrants to ISIS*, (Institute for Strategic Dialogue: London), strategicdialogue.org/ISDJ2969_Becoming_Mulan_01.15_WEB.PDF.
4 It should be noted that we do not communicate with the females we track. The reasoning for this is twofold; firstly, the vast majority of questions we would want answered about the conditions, roles and modalities of their migration, as well as the reasons that they went are addressed openly in their online accounts and blogs. Secondly, communication could put the female directly at risk.

from Britain, the Netherlands, Sweden, France and Germany and smaller numbers from Finland, Australia, Belgium, Canada, Austria, Norway, Bosnia and the United States.

56% of the women we track are currently married, most to foreign terrorist fighters with similar national or at least linguistic backgrounds. We know from our research that once in ISIS territory, linguistic groups tend to live in proximity to each other as most foreign recruits do not speak Arabic or local dialects.

As many as 30% of the women we track are already widowed. These numbers have increased significantly in the last 6 months. At least 13% of these women have shared, on their social media accounts, that they have children - with a number of them becoming pregnant while in ISIS territory. This number is likely to be much higher as many omit posting photos or writing about their children online for safety reasons.

The most striking feature of the dataset is the diversity of the profiles of these women. Female migrants that we track range from 14 to 46 years of age, though the majority are between 15 and 25 years of age. There is a large proportion of 16 year olds and, overall, we see the age of female recruits diminishing, with the youngest known recruit being a 13 year old girl from Germany. Indeed, Western female recruits are by and large younger than male recruits, in part as a function of ISIS' drive to recruit ever younger girls. Not only is there a greater need to supply wives for the thousands of foreign terrorist fighters from all over the world who have already joined ISIS, but also these men want women that speak their language while also being young enough to ensure they are unwed and 'untainted'.

While many women from the Middle East have travelled with husbands or families, the majority of the women we track from the West have gone as single females, often in pairs or within small groups. Ethnicities and family backgrounds vary, and while many come from a range of Muslim family backgrounds there is also a high rate of converts to Islam joining the movement[5]. Educational levels range from secondary school through high school and even post-graduate levels. While some of these women might be considered 'underprivileged', many others have high-level qualifications, including female doctors.

These factors are testament to the universal appeal of ISIS and the success of its highly sophisticated recruitment strategies. This diversity also highlights why it so difficult to draw an actionable profile of individuals that may be more vulnerable to ISIS recruitment.

---

[5] Looking at the Muslim population as a whole and % of radicalisation versus the group of converts as a whole and % of radicalisation, there is a higher rate of radicalisation among converts. globalecco.org/en_GB/ctx-v1n1/violent-converts-to-islam

3) Why is this happening? 'Pull vs. push' factors, 'Brand Caliphate' and the role of ideology

In my view, one of the reasons that so many years after the 9/11 and 7/7 attacks we still lack a coherent, strategic, international policy approach to the rising challenge of extremist recruitment is that there continues to be a lack of consensus over the drivers of radicalisation and the nature of the phenomenon that we are facing. While 'push factors' have received a great deal of attention over the years, 'pull factors' have been largely ignored.

Push factors

For a long time, governments viewed this problem largely through a socio-economic, integration or equalities lens. Yet, if economic inequality and social marginalisation were the primary drivers of extremism, the Roma community in Europe should pose the greatest terrorist challenge on the continent. Moreover, as our dataset shows, women who join ISIS defy easy categorisation on socio-economic grounds.

There is no question that Muslim millennials that have grown up in a post 9/11 media environment, in which Muslims and Islam are constantly 'bad news', are faced with a serious identity crisis and many young Muslims in the West will face discrimination and prejudice. This, often mixed with a set of foreign policy grievances, as well as personal traumas, feeds the vulnerabilities that extremists prey on.

Of the girls and women that we have been tracking, the most common grievances that they talk about as their drivers for leaving their home countries and emigrating to Syria can be categorised as follows:

1) Feeling isolated socially and/or culturally, including questioning their own identity and belonging within a Western culture;
2) Feeling that the international Muslim community or the 'ummah' is being violently persecuted; and
3) Resentment over the lack of international action in response to this persecution.

This is very much in line with the underlying male grievance narrative that 'nobody is doing anything to help our brothers and sisters in Syria, in Palestine, in the Central African Republic'. Historical revisionism brings a myriad of past and present conflicts under the simplified umbrella of 'Islam under attack'; of 'us versus them'.

For women, layers of identity-based questioning are added to this. What does it mean to belong, to be a Muslim female in a Western world? The Western 'emancipation' project is seen as a ruse, as a means to sexualise women. 'Look at *Victoria's Secret* and the role of women play as objects'. The so-called 'Islamic State' presents the opportunity to live free of such "tyranny"; the opportunity to gain solidarity, sisterhood, belonging and (self)-respect. Joining ISIS is presented to and among the women as an emancipator and as an empowering project.

'Push factors' - real and perceived grievances - while likely to make a person more vulnerable to the overtures of extremists and their propaganda, and important to address, is only part of the picture. Though they were placed at the centre of government responses for many years, 'push factors' on their own provide an incomplete and inadequate explanation of the widespread radicalisation and recruitment phenomenon we see today.

What has too often been missing from Western analysis, policy and operational responses is an understanding of the central role that an interlinked set of 'pull factors' play. While we recognise that ISIS represents a game-changing shift in the dynamics of violent extremism, our perspective on the rise of ISIS needs to be wider.

Strategic and tactical pull factors

Well before ISIS and the onset of the digital era, the vastly well-resourced global propaganda recruitment machine of Wahhabi Salafism, began making a play for the centre of gravity in Muslim culture and religious practice around the world. Gradually and insidiously it eradicated the expression of diverse, indigenous Islamic traditions and practices and sowed the intellectual foundations of the monolithic Islamist extremist movements we are facing today. This aggressive export and funding of an arcane ideology has gone essentially unchallenged for three decades, visibly changing cultural and religious practices around the world in a way that disproportionately affects women, and in many places sees girls, in particular, breaking with their mothers' and grandmothers' traditions.

That is why, despite differences in ethnic origins, Islamic traditions and practices, and despite differential levels of integration and equality - and indeed different foreign policy positions of governments – a common stream of Islamist extremism can be found everywhere today.

The role of the non-violent aspects of this ideology should also not be underestimated. We have seen that those Western countries in which Islamist extremist networks have been able to thrive most have proven to be the countries yielding the highest numbers of foreign terrorist fighters and female migrants. Al Muhajiroun in the UK, Ansar al Haqq in France and

Sharia for Belgium are just a few such examples of groups that toe the line of legality while mainstreaming extremist narratives.

The onset of the digital era has simply hyper-charged this propaganda recruitment machine. ISIS is the 'cherry on the cake', rather than the cake itself, and the 'elephant in the room' is the large-scale support emanating from the Gulf region for this ideological spread.

While, at the strategic level, this global ideological backdrop is essential to comprehend, at the tactical level the 'pull factors' consist of a mixture of 'Brand Caliphate' and the extremely sophisticated, tech savvy, communications machinery that ISIS has mounted.

From the iconic memes, to the go-pro footage from the field that mimics the imagery of popular video games, to the Twitter amplification apps and peer-to-peer - in this case, girl to girl - engagement that would be the envy of most social media marketing companies, ISIS has taken the Jihadist propaganda machine to the next level with obvious effect.

ISIS's has enabled decentralised messengers to spread their ideology through online and offline channels. By allowing decentralised voices – women, foreign fighters, supporters from any pocket of the world – to spread ISIS propaganda, the extremist message has become localised. Messaging is fluent, colloquial and turns local grievances into an international call to arms.

The internet has played a key role in increasing female participation in Jihadist groups. While they would have been excluded from the offline networks that once characterised Jihadist recruitment, the online world has provided women with an arena in which they can have real agency. ISIS has been particularly successful at leveraging that potential, supporting the prolific use of social media by ISIS women, especially Western women. ISIS has understood all too well the PR and recruitment value they represent.

As noted above, joining ISIS is seen as and represented by these women as a sort of emancipatory project. A 'jihadi girl-power' sub-culture has emerged on social media networks, clearly rooted in Western culture while simultaneously rejecting it. The propaganda image below clearly demonstrates this trend, parodying well-known Western beauty-industry advertisement campaigns.

As well as providing practical advice to girls about how to get to Syria, what to bring, and how to avoid the scrutiny of parents and security services, narratives about belonging and sisterhood are extremely prominent across the social media accounts of the women in our dataset and constitute an important part of the 'pull' narrative.

'Brand Caliphate'

But by far the most important 'pull' factor in the recruitment of women has been 'Brand Caliphate'. While a number of women travelled to Syria with their husbands in the early months of the Syrian conflict, it is only since the announcement of the Caliphate that we see numbers of unmarried women start to make the journey to Syria. That is because 'Brand Caliphate' represents more than just fighting. It represents the building of an 'Islamic Utopia' and as such it offers people a diversity of roles as part of its state building project.

This is heavily emphasised in ISIS statements. To women, their message is 'we praise your divine role as wife and mother to the next generation. You are not objects, we value you'. In ISIS's negotiations with the Jordanian government regarding the pilot they held hostage and later killed, they chose to demand the release of Sajida al-Rishawi, a women imprisoned on terrorist charges for an attempted suicide bombing attack linked to Al-Qaeda in Iraq, predecessor to ISIS. This was designed to send a very strong message to women about how ISIS values and protects its sisters.

The 'Caliphate' offers adventure, belonging and sisterhood, romance, spiritual fulfilment and a tangible role in idealistic utopia-building. Very few youth sub-cultures or movements can claim to offer so much.

The reality of the 'Caliphate' is what distinguishes ISIS from al-Qaeda and other jihadist organisations. The fact of occupying a geographical territory, which actually and purely manifests the ideology rather than merely ideals and hopes, is extremely significant. This territory has created a destination point, giving real-world credibility to ISIS's message.

4. The narrative vs. the reality on the ground

The social media output of female recruits living in ISIS territory gives us an important new lens into behavioural patterns, processes of radicalisation and community dynamics. This includes insights - though incomplete - into what life is like in ISIS territory. Platforms including Facebook, Twitter, Ask.fm, Instagram and Tumblr allow us to analyse not only the strategic role of women within ISIS but also give a better understanding as to why and how these individuals left their home countries and what roles females play once in ISIS territory. These insights are crucial in informing and improving policy, prevention methods and de-radicalisation approaches.

Once in the so-called 'Caliphate' women primarily play a domestic role. Women in ISIS territory are forbidden from leaving the confines of the home without supervision and pre-agreed permission. Their core responsibilities are to marry within a maximum of three months of their arrival, reproduce in order to populate the 'Caliphate', and to care for their husbands.

This reality seems contradictory to their activist online roles, the Jihadi girl-power sub-culture they espouse and the levels of brutality expressed in their communications. They are equally - if not more - violent than their male counterparts in their language online and are aggressive in their incitement of hatred and violence. To assume they were 'naïve' or 'ignorant' to ISIS' brutality would be incorrect. While the term 'jihadi brides' is an over-simplified term, women are not ignorant that their primary role will be to marry a jihadist and produce the next generation. This narrative alone plays on a sense of adventure embedded in the physical journey, as well as the promise of marrying a jihadist fighter, who offers his bride a place in paradise if killed in battle.

Despite their limited individual freedom of movement, women are given light military training, indicating that their roles could change in the future. Reports and research has also shown that they are given intensive religious training and some Arabic language training to immerse them in their new home. Certain groups of Turkish and Middle Eastern women have also been given more active roles, such as through the Al-Khansaa Brigade, in being morality police of other women, and even in carrying out violent punishments for women who are note conforming to their strict Shariah Law.

So while it is important to remember that many of these girls are minors and a type of grooming has been applied, it is equally clear that many of these women are genuinely committed ideologically to their cause. So, despite the violent pronouncements, the mass of images of fully-covered women baring firearms and the emancipatory narratives they share about leaving the West, they submit willingly to the largely domestic role women are allocated and to the martyrdom of their husbands. While it sometimes sounds reluctant, they remind each other of the structures they have committed themselves to, and warn would-be female recruits not to travel with the wrong expectations.

> *I have stressed this before on twitter but I really need sisters to stop dreaming about coming to Shaam and not getting married. Wallahi [I swear to God] life here is very difficult for the Muhajirat and we depend heavily on the brothers for a lot of support. It is not like the west where you can casually walk out and go to Asda/Walmart and drive back home ... even till now we have to stay safe outside and must always be accompanied by a Mahram [chaperone].*[71]

Post from: Umm Layth, 9 April 2014, http://fa-tubalilghuraba.tumblr.com [last accessed 28 November 2014]

5) Do these women matter? Are they a real threat?

To answer this question, we should be looking to the value they hold for ISIS.

Although ISIL currently prohibits women from engaging in warfare these women have been equally radicalised to glorify ISIL's violent endeavours, tweet, share and like the most gruesome of content and insight violence in others. Many have also openly discussed their own desires to participate in violence.

Examples of female migrants to ISIS wanting to participate in the violence:

Umm Ubaydah @FlamessOfwar, 20 November 2014
'So many beheadings at the same time, Allahu Akbar [God is the greatest],
this video is beautiful #DawlaMediaTeamDoingItRight'
https://twitter.com/FlamessOfwar [last accessed 28 November 2014]

Umm Irhab @MuslimahMujahi1, 20 August 2014
'I was happy to see the beheading of that kaafir [non-believer], I just rewinded
to the cutting part. Allahu akbar! [God is the greatest!] I wonder what was he
thinking b4 the cut'.
https://twitter.com/MuslimahMujahi1 [last accessed 28 November 2014]

Umm Ubaydah @FlamessOfwar, 10 October 2014
'my best friend is my grenade ... It's an American one too Lool. May Allah
allow me to kill their Kanzeer [pig] soldiers with their own weapons.'
https://twitter.com/FlamessOfwar [last accessed 28 November 2014]

Umm Khattab @UmmKhhattab_, 8 December 2014
'Laaawl me and the akhawats [sisters] thought maybe murtads [apostates]
were in the city lool I put the belt on and everything.'
https://twitter.com/UmmKhhattab__ [last accessed 8 December 2014]

This last one is in reference to her reaching for a possible suicide or grenade explosive belt
as she hears gunshots outside showing the willingness to react in a violent martyrdom
fashion.

New migration patterns

Jihadist strategy has always relied on asymmetrical warfare, changing tactics and movements to create a constantly shifting frontline. We are already witnessing the development of new migration patterns with Western female migrants. Just a fortnight ago, our researchers identified newly recruited women seemingly travel directly to ISIS-affiliate controlled areas in Libya rather than Syria and Iraq.

The three women were tracked to Libya. Two of them appear to be British, frequently mention other 'offline' peers, including women that live in the same compound as them. Two of these three are not yet married and it appears that all three travelled independently of each other, without familial relationships. One of these women appears to have been in ISIS-held areas of Libya since at least April this year.

ISIS's state-building efforts are scaling up and their attempts to expand the caliphate to regions with strong affiliate strongholds are already well underway. The recruitment of women to these areas is a firm part of that strategy.

6. What should we do to address this growing threat?

You cannot beat the challenge of radicalisation through drones and border measures. In order to have an impact on the conveyor belt of radicalisation and to 'drain the swamp' from which extremists recruit, we need to put in place a proportional soft-power competition strategy to close the gap that has emerged between their sophisticated, well-resourced, 24/7 global propaganda recruitment machinery and our response, which is not.

A quote of Osama bin Laden's from 2002 gives a clear indication of how centrally important propaganda is for extremist groups: "It is obvious that the media war in this century is one of the strongest methods. In fact, its ratio may reach 90% of the total preparation for the battles." During the Cold War, the need to invest in the soft-power battle of ideas was well understood. In the UK last year, we spent £40 million on prevention (and UK spending on 'prevention' trumps other European countries' spending). We spent $26 billion on training the Iraqi Army over the last decade.

A serious soft-power competition strategy cannot be limited to a series of Twitter campaigns and cannot be delivered through government counter-messaging centres. It needs to combine aid budgets with diplomatic efforts, bringing real muscle to the equation. In this way, countering extremism can be mainstreamed across different areas of international engagement.

We need to be clear about the objective of this soft-power strategy: it cannot simply be to reduce the number of individuals joining ISIS. It must be to redress the growing tide of support for, and sympathy with, the underpinning ideology of ISIS – and, by extension, the plethora of organisations, including al-Qaeda, which subscribe to that ideology. This means that we must work at both the immediate, tactical, hard edge of prevention and de-radicalisation and at the strategic level to counter the underlying ideology.

At a strategic level, we must work to undermine 'Brand Caliphate', which has done more for the Jihadi cause writ large, but also for female recruitment, than anything else. While there is clearly a geostrategic dimension to this, regardless of military outcomes, 'Brand Caliphate' needs to be exposed and delegitimised. From an intellectual, political and theological standpoint, those voices that can speak authoritatively about the heresy and inauthenticity of this 'Caliphate', as well about the real outcomes for Muslims living under its rule, must be uplifted. As part of this, we should be providing support to local individuals and groups trying, usually with little or no financial support, to protect indigenous cultural traditions, sites and heritage, to promote diversity within Islam against the monolithic vision propagated by the extremists.

Amplifying such perspectives and voices is an intrinsic part of confronting the extremist propaganda machinery which has gone unchallenged for so long. While governments have largely been focused on trying to get problematic material off the internet, our findings indicate that such 'take down' approaches tend not to be effective. The speed at which accounts get removed is very slow (this happens primarily through referral programmes by governments and now Europol to internet companies that then have the responsibility to remove content themselves), and the speed at which they get replaced under a different name or on a different platform is very fast.

Not only is this 'whack a mole' phenomenon not effective, but our research indicates that removal of accounts - censorship - may in fact increase the influence of extremists. In our database of ISIS women, the second accounts of women who have had their primary accounts taken down tend to have more followers.

Equally, as larger platforms like Facebook, Twitter and YouTube increase their take down measures, there is an online migration of extremist networks onto smaller, less regulated platforms, making surveillance and tracking all the more difficult. This is not to say that certain types of take down measures may not be effective. We are exploring the potential impact of removing whole social networks at once for instance. But, in my view, this can only ever be a partial response.

We need to focus more attention on competing actively with the extremists instead, engaging young people directly in a space that we have ceded to the extremists, and developing credible counter-narratives[6].

Credible voices are essential in reaching vulnerable, would-be recruits. There is evidence that survivors of extremist attacks, escapees and defectors can engage people flirting with extremist ideologies, as well as those that are already radicalised, in a more influential way than any other constituency. The Institute for Strategic Dialogue has built up and runs the largest global network of former extremists in the world, *Against Violent Extremism (AVE)*, in collaboration with Google Ideas and the GenNext Foundation. But more women are needed. It will be important to build out the network to include female defectors, escapees and survivors, and governments can help to asses and access returnees and defectors around the world.

However, while these stories and credible voices are important, on their own they tend not to have the tools or resources to reach the target audiences they would need to at scale or on an ongoing basis. As such, their influence is currently limited. We need therefore to build a civil society-led counter-narrative machinery to support the production and amplification of targeted, data-driven, counter-narrative campaigns and interventions, deployed with professionalised technology and communications support, just as the extremists' propaganda is. Data analytics must underpin this machinery, both to target audiences and to monitor the impact of campaigns on an ongoing basis, ensuring optimal and cost effective delivery. Perhaps most importantly, this is not a 'one size fits all' domain: different approaches are applicable depending on where people are along the radicalisation spectrum.

---

[6] See: R. Briggs and S. Feve (January 2014) *Policy Briefing: Countering the Appeal of Extremism Online* [strategicdialogue.org/Inspire_Radicalize_Recruit.pdf] and *Review of Programmes to Counter Narratives of Violent Extremism* [strategicdialogue.org/CounterNarrativesFN2011.pdf] (both Institute for Strategic Dialogue: London)

The Institute for Strategic Dialogue is trialling a range of campaigns and interventions through its counter-narrative *Innovation Hub*, bringing credible voices and ideas together with the creative, tech and communications capabilities needed to have impact.

Partnerships with Google, Facebook and Twitter have been critical in this domain. An earlier pilot programme run with YouTube saw counter-narrative material that was reaching only some 50 randomised users online turned into a campaign that engaged 50,000 targeted users (people searching for information about how to get to Syria for Jihad) in just 6 weeks. At the sharper end of the radicalisation spectrum, our *One2One Initiative* is connecting former extremists directly to young people expressing extremist views and sympathies on social media networks with a 30% positive engagement rate so far.

However, there is currently a major gap in counter-narratives and outreach targeting 'at risk' girls and women. We urgently need to develop messaging that specifically targets female audiences. Female returnees and defectors in particular could provide a powerful counter-narrative to the messaging of ISIS's female recruits. But to do this well we need to understand the dynamics of women in extremism better and research in this space is still in its infancy. There is a great need for more comprehensive data. While we have some insights into the phenomenon in the West, we have very little data and information coming from the regions around ISIS-controlled territory. Even within the West, figures are often fairly sporadic and out-dated. German intelligence reported at the end of June that 100 of the 700 German nationals in ISIS territory are women, with half of those women being younger than 25. The last estimate from the UK government on the number of women that travelled to join ISIS was 60 in October 2014; it is likely that this figure is now closer to 100-120. We need more consolidated, up to date data.

We must continue work to pinpoint the narratives that are drawing women into this movement in significant numbers so that we can develop targeted, relevant counter-narratives and counter-measures. And we need to have a better understanding of the connections between the wider social phenomena, including the homogenisation of religious and cultural practices around the world, and the rise of female extremist agency.

But, the ultimate key is to prevent processes of radicalisation in the first place and to inoculate the next generation against falling prey to extremist propaganda. That requires an educational approach that teaches critical thinking (specifically in relation to internet consumption), alongside programmes that sensitise young people to extremist propaganda. The Institute for Strategic Dialogue has worked with partners in the education sector to develop *Extreme Dialogue*, a critical thinking inoculation programme, combining hard-hitting emotional films based on the stories of former extremists and survivors of extremism with an online set of tools and guides for teachers and social workers to use in either formal or informal educational settings. This has been rolled out in Canada and will be introduced in Europe this year, but much more is needed, and governments can and should help to get such programmes distributed in schools and communities.

On a practical level, as this challenge grows, we also need more women acting as practitioners in the counter-terrorism, counter-extremism and de-radicalisation spaces. In particular, female case workers will be vital in managing the inflow of women returning from Syria and Iraq. The inclusion of female practitioners is not just an issue of equality. In de-radicalisation and prevention work, gender dynamics are important for the necessary cognitive openings. Male practitioners will not be able to engage with young females that are 'at risk' of radicalisation in the same way that fellow female practitioners can, not least because of the fundamentalist gender roles solidified within radicalisation processes.

We must comprehend extremists as social movements and, as such, women are central to both their adoption and rejection. We need to develop networks that intimately understand their local contexts; that are able to reach out to young women on a peer-to-peer basis; and that are empowered to work on countering violent extremism (CVE). We need to support role models within communities, exposing young women to new perspectives and opportunities. As such, we are working together with the convening power and support of the US Department of State's Bureau of Educational and Cultural Affairs (ECA) to bring together a network of women from around the world that are working on CVE. On June 8-9 2015, in partnership with the Center for Strategic and International Studies (CSIS), we convened the first global *Women and Extremism Summit* in Washington DC. More robust infrastructure and support needs to be given to women within the CVE sector and we hope this initiative will contribute to that end by helping to spur counter-narrative content that targets girls and women as well as address the research lacunae that still exist in his domain.

Finally, we must continue to argue for human rights for women in countries with extreme regimes in power. This is of importance in itself, but it also helps to avoid charges of selective application of the West's stated principles, and hypocrisy, even if only partially.

We are currently losing the battle of ideas. They have a significant head-start and enormous human and financial resourcing. However, we have a small window of opportunity to scale up the programmes and approaches we know work, and to supercharge the counter-narrative, creating the sort of communications competition strategy that will ultimately drown ISIS out on the internet and beyond.

Recommended Reading:

Available on the ISD website: **www.strategicdialogue.org/publications**

'Till Martyrdom Do Us Part' Gender and the ISIS Phenomenon

Erin Marie Saltman & Melanie Smith, May 2015

Representing the second instalment of our Women and Extremism (WaE) programme, this report explores the phenomenon of Western females travelling to Syria and Iraq in support of ISIS. It first elaborates upon the motivations for these women and girls to migrate, explores some of the diverse range of profiles that have been monitored, and clarifies the role that they are likely to encompass once arriving in ISIS-held territory. Additionally, the report aims to elucidate how current government prevention and de-radicalisation infrastructure may be adapted to deal with this trend.

Becoming Mulan? Female Western Migrants to ISIS

Carolyn Hoyle, Alexandra Bradford and Ross Frenett, January 2015

Launching our Women and Extremism (WAE) programme, this report focuses on those women that have travelled from the West to ISIS held territory in support of the terrorist organisation. The first in a series of reports, this research draws on our database of known female migrants to ISIS and analyses their reasons for joining the group, the threat they pose and how to stem the flow of women joining ISIS.

Chairman ROYCE. Thank you.

To begin Mr. Watts' testimony, I think we are going to show a brief clip from his documentary Escaping ISIS. So we will see if that works.

[Video played.]

STATEMENT OF MR. EDWARD WATTS, DIRECTOR AND PRODUCER, ESCAPING ISIS

Mr. WATTS. Thank you, Mr. Chairman, and distinguished members of the committee, for the opportunity to testify today. For the last 6 months, as has been said, I have been working on this film called Escaping ISIS in the U.S., Escape from ISIS in the UK, that explores what life is like for an estimated 4 million women living under the rule of this Islamic State group.

I believe it is the most important subject I have covered in my career, and I am very glad the committee has made it the focus of this special hearing.

The treatment of women by ISIS is sometimes overshadowed by the terror group's more spectacular atrocities, yet I would argue no other section of society suffers more on a day-to-day basis at their hands. In the course of my work, I documented ISIS's abduction of thousands of non-Muslim women and girls, their sexual enslavement, and even the rape of girls as young as nine.

I gathered testimony that described markets where ISIS trade young women like cattle, or even rent them to each other for a few hundred dollars. They crimes are condoned, even celebrated, by ISIS's official publications. And it is important to remember that Muslim women, too, endure terrible oppression.

They are subject to severe limitations on their freedom of movement and right to education and work. They must abide by a strict dress code enforced through harsh physical punishments. Some are coerced into marriage to ISIS fighters; others have been stoned to death on trumped up charges of adultery. This should be the stuff of history books, not contemporary news reports.

It is worth noting as well that ISIS's extreme interpretation of Islam is not shared by the majority of Muslims in the territory under their control. Yet disturbingly I met a woman who had been forced to join the organization and then subsequently so thoroughly brainwashed that she now shared ISIS's vision for society, even to the point of punishing others who defied it. And we know, as Ms. Havlicek said, that young women from our own nations have been targeted for similar indoctrination and lured to the territory under the extremist control.

Such stories show that this is a struggle not only with the terrorist organization but also a system of ideas, one that threatens the principles on which our modern society is based. It is understandable that from afar we may feel powerless to stop these atrocities, but there is action we could take.

As you have seen, during the course of filming I met a number of local activists who with almost no outside support were risking their lives to undermine ISIS's rule and save the women and girls they can reach. Those activists could use our help, and we could do more to support the rehabilitation of women who come back, often with severe psychological and physical trauma.

The example of those survivors and activists should inspire us to reevaluate our policies and ask what more we can do. Renewed action is not only necessary but urgent. Every day that ISIS exists, more women will suffer horrendous violence or sexual assault, and more people will be subject to indoctrination in their ideas.

The fight against ISIS is all of our fight. It will require time, effort, and sacrifice on our part, too. But in ending their regime, we all stand to gain.

Thank you.

[The prepared statement of Mr. Watts follows:]

Statement by Edward Watts
Documentary Film-maker

U.S. House of Representatives Committee on Foreign Affairs
Special Hearing
July 29, 2015

"Women Under ISIS Rule: From Brutality to Recruitment"

Mr Chairman and Members of the Committee,

Thank you for the opportunity to testify before you today.

For the last six months I have been working on a film entitled *Escaping ISIS* that explores what life is like for the estimated four million women living under the rule of the Islamic State group. I believe it is the most important subject I have covered in my career. I am glad the Committee has made it the focus of this special hearing.

The treatment of women by ISIS is sometimes overshadowed by the terror group's more spectacular atrocities. Yet I would argue no other section of society suffers more on a day-to-day basis at their hands.

In the course of my work, I documented ISIS's abduction of thousands of non-Muslim women and girls, their sexual enslavement and the rape of girls as young as nine. I gathered testimony that described markets where ISIS trade young women like cattle, or even rent them to each other for a few hundred dollars. These crimes are condoned – even celebrated – by ISIS's official publications.

And Muslim women too endure terrible oppression.

They are subject to severe limitations on their freedom of movement and right to education and work; they must abide by a strict dress code enforced through harsh physical punishments; some are coerced into marriage to ISIS fighters; others have been stoned to death on trumped up charges of adultery.

This should be the stuff of history books, not contemporary news reports.

It's worth noting that ISIS's extreme interpretation of Islam is not shared by the majority of Muslims in the territory under their control. Yet, disturbingly, I also met women who had been so thoroughly brainwashed they now shared ISIS's vision for society, even to the point of punishing others who defy it. And we know that young women from our own nations have been targeted for similar indoctrination and lured to the territory under the extremists' control.

Such stories show that this is a struggle not only with a terrorist organisation but also a system of ideas, one that threatens the principles on which modern society is based.

It is understandable that, from afar, we may feel powerless to stop the atrocities. But there is action we could take. During the course of filming, I met a number of local activists who, with little outside support, were risking their lives to undermine ISIS's rule and save the women and girls they can reach.

Those activists could use our help. And we could do more to support the rehabilitation of women who come back, often with severe psychological and physical trauma.

The example of the survivors and activists should inspire us to re-evaluate our policies and ask what more we can do.

Renewed action is not only necessary, but urgent. Every day that ISIS exists, more women will suffer horrendous violence or sexual assault and more people will be subject to indoctrination in their ideas.

The fight against ISIS is all of our fight. It will require time, effort and sacrifice on our part too. But in ending their regime, we all stand to gain.

Thank you.

Edward Watts

Chairman ROYCE. Thank you, Edward.
Dr. Kuehnast.

STATEMENT OF KATHLEEN KUEHNAST, PH.D., DIRECTOR, GENDER AND PEACEBUILDING, CENTER FOR GOVERNANCE, LAW AND SOCIETY, UNITED STATES INSTITUTE OF PEACE

Ms. KUEHNAST. Good morning, and thank you, Chairman Royce and Ranking Member Engel, for this opportunity to testify before you today on an important and timely subject.

As ISIS captures land, resources, and people, it has borrowed a page out of the history book of other wars where deploying sexual violence destroyed families, communities, and the very moral fiber of a society.

When sexual violence is used in war, or by extremist groups to achieve their ends, it can be even more devastating than a gun. Major General Patrick Cammaert, a retired U.N. force commander in Eastern Congo, said that sexual violence is cheaper than a bullet and far more effective in its efforts to destroy an individual, a group, or a society.

How best should the United States Government respond to these horrifying accounts out of ISIS-controlled areas? Sexual violence and conflict must be seen by Congress and in U.S. foreign policy as a security issue. It is not simply a women's issue, even though many of its victims are women. It cannot be solved by women alone, nor can prevention happen in isolation.

Through U.N. security resolutions like 1325 and 1820, and our own U.S. National Action Plan on Women, Peace, and Security, sexual violence is framed as a peace and security issue. For the sake of this testimony, sexual violence includes acts of individual rape, gang rape, sexual slavery, sexual torture, genital mutilation, and sexual humiliation. Its victims are all ages, men and women, boys and girls.

For women and girls, the results of sexual violence perpetrated individually or on mass scale by ISIS results in isolation, exclusion, suicide, and, in the case of some parts of Iraq, murder by a family member in order to ''preserve the family's honor.'' There is no easy path to healing from rape and sexual violence and conflict. It is a long-term process and must be an integral and formal part of reconciliation in post-conflict situation.

A year ago, I testified before this committee on engaging and educating women and girls in the prevention of violent extremism. I emphasized, in addition to supporting girls going to school, we must strategically engage fathers, brothers, and sons in learning about gender equality to further enable a more capable and inclusive state, and to help end violence as a means of resolving conflict.

In the same way, policymaking community needs analysis and programming on how to help societies that have fused manhood and violence together as we see going on in ISIS today. Truly, this is a rite of passage issue. If the only way to become an adult male in your society is through a right of passage involving violence and war, then the chances for peace and security are significantly reduced.

It is alarming the way ISIS is reaching into the hearts and minds of very young people even under the age of 14 years of age, to entice them with promises of belonging and a violent sense of power over women and girls. This issue is why I believe the next security and peacebuilding challenge deserving our full attention is on children, peace, and security. It identifies both the humanitarian services and protections needed for boys and girls in war and in refugee camps.

Over the past year, reports have emerged that ISIS is setting their sights on young children. In March of this year, the London-based monitoring group, the Syrian Observatory for Human Rights, reported that ISIS had recruited at least 400 children this year. They refer to them as "tiny terrorists." Children are used in combat missions to execute prisoners and spies, families and neighborhoods, and markets and schools. Yes, it does remind us of another era of the Nazi generation of young recruits.

Because we are not collecting complete datasets on boys and girls, we are not fully tracking ISIS recruitment efforts. The Observatory reports boys as young as six are recruited into the "Cubs of the Lions" of the Caliphate. The boys are lured with the idea of money and weapons, shipped off to camps where they learn to shoot rifles. First, they learn to behead dolls, and then they execute human hostages.

For girls, the tactic of sexual violence takes the form of kidnapping girls, enslaving them, reselling them as "child brides." There is nothing childlike about these brides, and there is nothing bridelike about an enslaved girl.

The reality of ISIS trolling for children is something that should cause us great anxiety. We have inadequate data to fully understand what is happening in front of our very eyes. If we are to fight this trend, we need better data, how many children are being recruited, what is happening to them in the camps, can they be rescued and returned to society.

Years ago, I spent a summer working with 5- and 6-year-olds, Protestants and Catholics, in Northern Ireland during the troubles. I learned every night how early hatred is taught. I learned that vengeance even helps children rationalize the kind of violence that they have lived through. Such narratives of hate are now easily conveyed through social media.

At a recent conference at USIP on women encountering violent extremism, Mrs. Bangura with the U.N. stated that ISIS is using modern communications in the service of a Medieval agenda. She stressed, "Information is ISIS's oxygen, and we must suffocate them."

By employing the best of the free world's technology, ironically, ISIS has infiltrated social platforms like Facebook and Twitter. And, believe me, I am the mom of twin girls who are 14, and they have access to all of this information. It is startling. It is not just happening over there.

Indeed, a greater emphasis must be placed on children, especially those growing up in refugee crisis. It is worth remembering that there are more displaced people in the world today than anytime since World War II. The U.N. refugee agency reported last year that it has exceeded 50 million people. This includes many, many children.

ISIS is paying families for their boys to pick up a gun and their girls for sexual slavery. What kind of alternatives can be offered to the families so that children can pick up a pencil and learn while they are in these camps? We need to teach critical thinking skills. It is not enough to read; we need to help them understand how to think through the challenges that they face at a very young age.

Finally, we need age-sensitive ''exit ramps'' for children and youth who have been entangled in the web of ISIS control and brainwashing. We need to recognize that refugee children need food for their minds as well as food for their bodies. We need to encourage greater education at these refugee camps.

Ideally, the very, very best trauma counseling and healing assistance is necessary for victims of sexual violence and witnesses of that sexual violence. Otherwise, we stitch the violent experiences and memories into the DNA of this very young generation.

As the largest age cohort of children living on this planet approach their adolescent rights of passage to adulthood, we need to find ways to inspire and expand the free world as ISIS tries to offer shortcuts to a violent adulthood. We know all too well that violence is the shortest path to losing a childhood, a vision, and the way forward.

Thank you very much for your time.

[The prepared statement of Ms. Kuehnast follows:]

United States Institute of Peace

. . .

An independent institution established by Congress to strengthen the nation's capacity
to promote peaceful resolution to international conflicts

. . .

"Women Under ISIS Rule:
From Brutality to Recruitment"

Testimony before the House Foreign Affairs Committee
U.S. House of Representatives

Dr. Kathleen Kuehnast
United States Institute of Peace

July 29, 2015

Good morning and thank you to the House Foreign Affairs Committee Chairman Royce and Ranking Member Engel, and other Members of the Committee, for this opportunity to testify before you today on this important and timely subject: "Women under ISIS Rule: From Brutality to Recruitment."

My name is Dr. Kathleen Kuehnast. I am a socio-cultural anthropologist and direct Gender and Peacebuilding at the United States Institute of Peace. The U.S. Congress created the Institute 30 years ago with a mandate to prevent, mitigate and resolve violent conflicts around the world. The Institute does so by engaging directly in conflict zones and by providing analysis, education and resources to those working for peace. USIP experts work on the ground in some of the world's most volatile regions, collaborating with U.S. government agencies, non-governmental organizations, and local communities to foster peace and stability.

My statement reflects my own views, and does not necessarily represent the views of the U.S. Institute of Peace. The Institute does not take positions on policy and is prohibited in its statue from taking positions on legislation.

The Situation Today

Sexual violence must be seen by Congress and in U.S. foreign policy as a security issue. It is not simply a women's issue although many of its victims are women. Through UN Security Council Resolutions like 1325 and 1820, sexual violence is framed as a peace and security issue. For the sake of this testimony, sexual violence may include individual rape, gang rape, sexual slavery, sexual torture, genital mutilation and sexual humiliation.

How best should the US Government respond to the horrifying accounts coming out of ISIS-controlled areas?

Mr. Watts in his intense film brings the viewer face to face with the brutal treatment of women by ISIS. The recounting of the selling, raping, and stoning of women and girls acts not only as a witness to this human atrocity but is also a compelling counter argument for young people contemplating joining what can be described as a medieval-style gang.

Dr. Ahram describes how sexual violence is a systematic crime that targets children, boys and girls under 15 years of age. At an age when children are seeking affiliation and sorting out their identities, ISIS is attacking the society in order to destroy the ties of kinship and rearrange the lines of loyalty.

Ms. Havlicek takes us into the minds of international girls who are enticed into a web of evil. ISIS uses imagery of empowered women and manipulates them for their extremist cause and a sense of belonging to their movement.

Each of these experts' contributions is critical to understanding the current situation.

Sexual Violence is a Security Issue

When sexual violence is used in war or by extremists' groups to achieve their ends, it can be even more devastating than a gun. Major General Patrick Cammaert, a retired UN force commander in Eastern Congo, said that "sexual violence is cheaper than a bullet, and far more effective" in its efforts to destroy an individual, a group, or a society.

As ISIS captures land, resources, and people, it has borrowed a page out of the history of other wars where deploying sexual violence destroyed families, communities and the moral fiber of a society.

Impact on Society

For women and girls, the results of sexual violence, perpetrated individually or on a mass scale by ISIS, can include social exclusion, isolation, or even suicide. Or in the case of some Muslim societies like Iraq, murder by a family member in order to, quote, preserve the family's honor, unquote. There is no easy path to healing from rape and sexual violence. It is a long-term process and must be a part of the healing and reconciliation in post-conflict situations.

Although women and girls are more often the target of sexual violence, in some armed conflicts men and boys are also victims. Male rape is much more a taboo in many societies, and thus is rarely addressed in reintegration and reconciliation efforts after the conflict.

Sexual violence in conflict is a peace and security issue. It cannot be resolved by women alone. Nor can healing happen in isolation. It must be an inclusive effort of the society in which victims and survivors live.

Therefore, our work at the U.S. Institute of Peace defines gender as the dynamic relationship between men and women, and masculine and feminine identities. This dynamic is especially relevant in states experiencing violent conflict.

It is essential to define security concerns through a full gender lens. As Texas A & M political scientist Valerie Hudson notes, there is a direct correlation between countries where gender equality exists and more peaceful states and stable economies.

Last year when I testified before this Committee on "Engaging and Educating Women and Girls in the Prevention of Violent Conflict and Violent Extremism," I emphasized that it is not enough to support girls going to school. We must also engage fathers, brothers and sons in learning about gender equality, to further enable a more capable and more inclusive state. But also to help end violence as a means of resolving conflict.

In the same way, the policymaking community needs analysis and programming on how to help societies that have fused "manhood" and "violence" together. If the only way to become an adult male in your society is through a rite of passage involving violence and war, then the chances for peace and security are significantly reduced. The impact for women of this hyper masculine notion of manhood can be devastating.

A Focus on Children

It is alarming the way extremists' groups are reaching into the hearts and minds of very young men, under 14 years of age, to entice them with promises of belonging, and a violent sense of power over women and girls.

That's why I believe the next security and peacebuilding arena deserving of our full attention is Children, Peace and Security.

This identifies both the humanitarian services and protections needed for boys and girls in every kind of war and every type of refugee camp, and also the need to fight those who would make children the weapons of a new war.

Over the past year, reports have emerged that ISIS is less interested in youth over 14 years of old. Instead, they are setting their sights on young children. This includes using the tactic of sexual violence in the form of kidnapping girls, enslaving them, and reselling them. Boys are used as armed fodder-- as human bombs and executioners.

In March of this year, the London-based monitoring group, the Syrian Observatory for Human Rights, reported that ISIS has recruited at least 400 children this year — far more than the number of new adult recruits. ISIS refers to them as "tiny terrorists." Children are used to execute prisoners, in combat missions and as spies in families and neighborhoods, markets and schools.

Children are more malleable than young adults. They offer less resistance when threatened with violent acts of terrorism on their communities, on their family members and, on their bodies and minds. We must also recognize that children are able to find a way out of horrific human conditions. Yet, they can also take the opposite path and directly engage in violent acts.

Because we are not collecting complete data on girls and boys, we are not fully tracking this ISIS recruitment effort. The Observatory reports that "boys as young as six are recruited into "Ashbal al- Khilafah," which translates to "the Cubs of Lions of the Caliphate." The UK's Quilliam Foundation, an anti-extremist think tank, compares it to Hitler's Youth program—a core ideological and military training for hate.

The boys — often lured in with bribes of money and weapons — are shipped off to camps where they learn how to shoot rifles. They learn to behead dolls first, and then to execute human hostages.

The reality of ISIS trolling for children is something that should cause us all great anxiety. We have inadequate data to fully understand what is happening in front of our eyes. And we are only beginning to understand the online and social platform recruiting methods targeted to children. If we are to fight this trend, we need better data on how many children are being recruited or snatched, what is happening to them in these camps, and how they can be rescued and returned to society.

In 1980, I spent time at Corrymeela, a reconciliation camp in Northern Ireland during the troubles. Every night five and six year old Protestants and Catholics alike would tell me their stories of terror. I learned how early hatred is taught. I learned that vengeance helps even young children rationalize violence.

Such narratives of hate are now so easily conveyed through social media. A week ago, the U.S. Institute of Peace along with USAID and the Department of State hosted a conference on Women and Countering Violent Extremism. One of the keynote speakers, UN Special Representative on Sexual Violence in Conflict, Zainab Bangura, stated that ISIS is using modern communications in service of a "medieval agenda." She stressed, "Information is ISIS's oxygen, and we must suffocate them." By employing the best of the free world's technology, ironically ISIS has infiltrated social platforms like Facebook and Twitter and is recruiting young people every day.

Indeed, one of the White House Countering Violent Extremism work streams focuses on youth, and this is critical. These civil society reports, however, suggest that more is needed – both data as well as interventions – and greater focus should be on children under 14 years of age. This is especially pertinent when in terms of the growing refugee crisis.

It is worth remembering that there are more displaced people in the world today than any time since World War II. The UN refugee agency reported in 2014 that the number of refugees, asylum-seekers and internally displaced people worldwide has exceeded 50 million people. And this includes many, many children.

Idleness among boys and girls in refugee camps is dangerous. We must more fully engage kids in active, creative learning. If ISIS is paying families for their boys to pick up a gun, and their girls to be captured for sexual slavery or as child brides, what kinds of alternatives can be offered to the families so that children can pick up a pencil and learn while they are in these camps? We need to be looking at ways to engage children with critical analysis and a skill set that leads them away from ISIS, not toward it.

Unless the international community, led by the U.S., tackles the massive and growing refugee crisis head on, these children will grow up without the capacity to ever become engaged citizens.

We are at that pivotal point in history. We are at an urgent reckoning of the human condition as we see the rapid decrease of safe spaces for civil society to operate within. At the same time, ISIS is all about building a new world -- a world that looks to us more like the Dark Ages with its use of ancient torture and violent acts ISIS has made it its mission to enslave women and girls as a key strategy toward building this new world order. And sexual violence is at the heart of their tactics.

Recommendations

The U.S. needs to demonstrate action moving forward.

- Recognize that children need food for their minds as well as food for their bodies. Encourage greater attention to education in refugee camps as a step in that direction.

- Develop age-sensitive "exit" ramps for children and youth who have been entangled in the web of ISIS's control and brainwashing.

- Develop ideally the very best trauma counseling and healing assistance possible for all the victims of sexual violence. All the family members who have had to stand witness to these horrific crimes deserve a chance to heal.

- U.S. policymakers should consider how U.S. security will be enhanced by even modest efforts to combat the ability of extremists to recruit children and to perpetrate sexual violence.

- The U.S. should lead a global effort to create the tools, resources and experts to address the deep physical and mental trauma inflicted on a generation of young people. Otherwise, we will stitch the violent experiences and memories into the DNA of this young generation.

As the largest age cohort of children living on this planet approach their adolescent rites of passage to adulthood, we need to find ways to inspire and expand the free world; as ISIS tries to offer shortcuts to a violent adulthood.

We know all too well that violence is the shortest path to losing a childhood, a vision, and the way forward.

The views expressed in this testimony are those of the author and not the U.S. Institute of Peace, which does not take policy positions.

Chairman ROYCE. Thank you.

Dr. Ahram, you have 5 minutes.

STATEMENT OF ARIEL AHRAM, PH.D., ASSISTANT PROFESSOR, VIRGINIA TECH SCHOOL OF PUBLIC AND INTERNATIONAL AFFAIRS

Mr. AHRAM. Thank you, Mr. Chairman, and the committee, for the opportunity to speak about the catastrophic sexual violence occurring in Syria and Iraq today. I use the word "catastrophic" to stress to you the magnitude of the crisis. The Islamic State has systematically abducted, enslaved, and sexually terrorized thousands, and likely tens of thousands, of women and girls.

There are two common but equally unhelpful perspectives on this situation. The first is to see ISIS as a unique collection of religiously crazed thugs. The second is to dismiss sexual violence as a natural and inevitable byproduct of the civil war enveloping Syria and Iraq today.

Research by Dara Cohen and Ragnhild Nordas show that sexual violence is common in many but hardly all civil wars. Rape is particularly prevalent when fighting groups have trouble recruiting combatants or rely on contraband to finance their operations. Rape can be part of an operational culture, even if it is not specifically ordered by commanders. With that in mind, it is important to consider ISIS's sexual violence not just in the context of the war that ISIS is fighting but also the kind of state that ISIS is building.

Three types of sexual violence are especially noteworthy. The first is sexual enslavement of women and girls. Sexual enslavement is uniquely reserved for sectarian groups, which ISIS considers to be apostate or heretical to Islam—Shi'is, Alawais, Yazidis, Druze, Shabak, Baha'is, and Sunni Muslims that differ from ISIS's religious interpretations.

ISIS selectively cites Islamic jurists to justify treating people from these groups as spoils, essentially property. They are raped at will. Captured women are enslaved in brothels and sold on the street, yielding a revenue stream to ISIS. Sexual enslavement is also part of a process of ethno-sectarian annihilation.

Besides immense physical harm, sexual violence induces dishonor and shame among its victims. Even if they escape, former captives are often considered despoiled and ineligible for marriage, in effect preventing whole generations from procreating.

There are many reports of suicide and honor killings. Perversely, this type of sexual violence yields another strategic benefit to ISIS. Children born from such rape are generally considered to be Sunni Muslims and, therefore, augment ISIS's demographic base.

The second type of sexual violence is forced marriage of women and girls. Unlike sexual enslavement, marriage entails reciprocal obligations through dowries. These marriages turn ISIS members into "one of the family," so to speak. ISIS's predecessor, al-Qaeda in Mesopotamia, tried to extort tribal sheikhs in western Iraq to marry their daughters to ISIS fighters. Many sheikhs apparently resisted this, a factor which motivated tribes to join the Awakening movement.

Keeping in mind that ISIS permits polygamy and child marriage, we have no idea about the wishes of the women themselves. Today,

ISIS continues to build networks through forced marriage and operates marriage bureaus to find spouses for male fighters. Foreign fighters are reputed to offer bridal prices in the tens of thousands of dollars.

The promise of finding an eligible spouse has been an element in ISIS's effort to attract foreigners, both men and women. For those caught in the war zone, marrying into ISIS may seem a way to ensure protection for themselves and their families.

Thirdly is ISIS's sexual violence against men and boys. ISIS has tortured and killed accused homosexuals in especially horrifying ways. There are also sketchy reports of ISIS sodomizing adolescent boys as part of an initiation or induction of child soldiers. This is consistent with other cases where sexual violence induces shame, and, therefore, increases barriers to exit should a recruit try to flee.

ISIS's brazen and systematic campaign of sexual violence represents a crime against humanity and is widely reviled in the West and in the Islamic world. However, ISIS is not the only belligerent to carry out sexual violence. Other rebel groups, as well as Iraqi, Kurdish, and Syrian security forces, have also used sexual violence, including rape and sexual torture.

Recognizing this gives a better appreciation of how Sunni Arabs might view ISIS as a defender of their interests. It also underscores the point that ISIS is not the sole cause of the crisis.

What can be done to help the situation? I fear that a military response will likely produce even more population displacement and leave more women and children vulnerable to sexual exploitation, at least in the short term.

There are, instead, a number of non-military measures that can help ameliorate the crisis. The first is to aid neighboring states to stop the flow of human trafficking in their countries. The second is to pressure Syria and Iraq to stop using sexual violence themselves. This would include the activities of pro-government militias like the Popular Mobilization Forces and the National Defense Units in Syria.

Finally, the U.S. must support the United Nations and NGOs working directly with victims of sexual violence. These efforts will be crucial in assisting victims reintegrate with their communities.

Thank you.

[The prepared statement of Mr. Ahram follows:]

Testimony before United States House Committee on Foreign Affairs
"The Islamic State's War on Women and Girls"
Wednesday, July 29, 2015
Rayburn House Office Building, Room 2170

Ariel I. Ahram, Ph.D.
Associate Professor
Virginia Tech School of Public and International Affairs

Thank you Chairman Royce and the committee for the opportunity to speak to you today about the catastrophic levels of sexual violence that has occurred in the midst of the civil wars in Syria and Iraq. Please note that my comments here reflect only my own views, not those of Virginia Tech or any other organization. Also, with your permission, I wish to submit an expanded written statement for the record.

I use the word catastrophic deliberately in order to stress to you the magnitude of the crisis today engulfing Iraq and Syria. The Islamic State in Iraq and Syria (ISIS) has systematically abducted, enslaved, and sexually terrorized thousands — and likely tens of thousands — of women and girls. There are two equally unhelpful tendencies when it comes to understanding sexual violence of this nature. The first is to see ISIS as a unique collection of religiously-crazed thugs and sociopaths. The second is to dismiss sexual violence as a natural and inevitable byproduct of war. Extensive research by Dara Cohen at Harvard's Kennedy School of Government and Ragnhild Nordås at the Peace Research Institution, Oslo has found that sexual violence is common in many — but hardly all — civil wars. Rape is particularly prevalent when fighting groups have trouble recruiting combatants or rely on contraband to finance their operations, factors which tend to decrease fighting discipline and worsen treatment of civilians generally. Rape can become part of the operational culture of both rebel and state forces, even if it is not specifically ordered or sanctioned from commanders at the top.

With that in mind, it is important to consider ISIS's sexual violence not just in the context of the war that ISIS is fighting, but also the kind of state that ISIS purports to be building. As Valerie Hudson, a professor at Texas A&M's Bush School of Government and Public Service, and Patricia Ledl, a former advisor to the United Nations and USAID, point out in their most recent book, "a social order based on the subordination of women will always subjugate all but the most powerful men." Several different different forms of sexual violence are noteworthy, creating different kinds of subordination and hierarchy within the Islamic State:

1. First is sexual enslavement. This type of sexual violence has understandably gained the most attention. Sexual enslavement is uniquely reserved for sectarian groups which ISIS considers to be apostate or heretical to Islam. This includes Shi'is of all denomination, Alawis, Yezidis, Shabak, Druze, Baha'is, and Sunni Muslims that differ from ISIS's religious interpretations. The exact status of Christians, Jews and others considered "Peoples of the Book" is unclear. ISIS selectively cites medieval Islamic jurists to justify treating people from these groups as spoils, essentially property. They are raped at will. There is a profit motive to this kind of sexual violence. Captured women are enslaved in

ISIS-run brothels and sold on the street in Mosul, Raqqa, and elsewhere. Sexual enslavement is also part of a process of ethno-sectarian annihilation. Besides immense physical harm, sexual violence induces dishonor and shame among its victims and their families. ISIS's female captives are often considered despoiled and ineligible for marriage, in effect ruining families and preventing whole generations from procreating. There are reports of ISIS forcing captured Yezidi women to describe their victimization to their families by phone. There are also reports of honor-killings and suicide. Perversely, this type of sexual violence yields another strategic benefit for ISIS. Children born from such rape are generally considered by ISIS doctrine to be Sunni Muslim. They therefore augment the demographic base of the Islamic State itself.

2. The second type of sexual violence is forced marriage. Unlike sexual enslavement, marriage entails reciprocal obligations through the dowry and other kinds of exchange. These marriages help knit together the ISIS community through consanguine ties, turning ISIS members into "one of the family," so to speak. ISIS's predecessor, Al-Qaeda in Mesopotamia, tried to extort tribal sheikhs in western Iraq to marry their daughters to ISIS fighters in the mid-2000s. Many sheikhs apparently resisted this, a factor which motivated tribes to join the Awakening movement. We, of course, have no idea about the wishes of the women themselves. Today ISIS continues to try to build networks through forced marriage, bearing in mind that ISIS permits polygamy in conformation to Islamic law. ISIS operated marriage bureaus or brokerages to find spouses for their male fighters. Foreign fighters are reputed to offer bridal prices in the tens of thousands of dollars, in effect gaining citizenship in the Islamic State through marriage. The promise of finding an eligible Muslim spouse has been an element in ISIS's effort to attract foreigners, both men and women. For those caught in the war zone, marrying into ISIS may seem a way to ensure protection for themselves and their families.

3. Third, I would be remiss if I did not also mention ISIS's practices of sexual violence against males. ISIS has tortured and killed accused homosexuals in especially gruesome and horrifying ways. There are also sketchy reports that sexual violation is part of ISIS's practices for initiation or induction of adolescent recruits. Just as for women, these acts induce profound shame and stigmatization in the victim. This use of sexual violence appears consistent with other cases of civil wars where sexual violence against child soldiers increases barriers to exit should a recruit try to flee and thus helps to solidify unit cohesion.

ISIS is brazen and systematized in its campaign of sexual violence. Collectively these actions represent crimes against humanity and violations of the laws of war. They are widely and justly reviled in the West and in the Islamic world.

However, ISIS is not the only belligerent in Syrian-Iraqi civil wars to carryout sexual violence. International human rights organizations have documented how Iraqi, Kurdish, and Syrian security forces have used sexual violence, including sexualized torture and rape. Pro-government militia groups, such as the National Defense Battalions in Syria and the Popular Mobilization Units in Iraq, have been implicated in rape and other atrocities against civilians. Recognizing the extent and scope of sexual violence gives a better appreciation for the perception by some in the Sunni communities that ISIS offers them defense against brutalization. It also reinforces the crucial point that ISIS is not the sole cause for the violence enveloping the region.

What can be done to help the situation? I fear that a military response will likely generate more violence and induce greater population displacement. Displaced populations are the most vulnerable to all kinds of sexual exploitation, including abductions, enslavement, and prostitution. In 2013 alone the United Nations Population Fund had received request for assistance from 38,000 Syrians related to gender-based violence, including rape, domestic violence, and abuse. As the number of refugees and IDPs has ballooned, this number has almost certain grown as well.

The U.S. has a number of non-military measures that can help alleviating the crisis of sexual violence. The first is to aid Turkey, Jordan, and Saudi Arabia, and other regional states to stop the flow of human trafficking in their areas in order cut off the financial benefits that come from sexual enslavements. Secondly, the U.S. can also put pressure on Syrian and Iraqi authorities to stop using sexual violence themselves. This would help to reassure frightened Sunni communities and keep them from turning to ISIS for protection. Finally and most importantly, the U.S. must support UNHCR and international and local NGOs working directly with the victims of sexual violence in Lebanon, Jordan, Turkey, Iraq, and elsewhere. The efforts of these agencies will be crucial to assist sexual violence victims reintegrate with their communities and mitigate the stigma attached to victimization.

Thank you.

Chairman ROYCE. Thank you. I was going to ask you a question, Doctor, just about the reality that, despite the brutality, you read these cases where they actually convince local girls to adopt their extremist views. Can you maybe explain that process to me?

Mr. AHRAM. ISIS relies a great deal on knowledge of the local conditions for its operations. The core of ISIS is derived from Sunni Arab tries in western Iraq. They understand the local mores, and often those local mores are quite conservative to begin with. And so the proposition that women should remain covered, that they should stay in the house, that does not seem as alien to people in those areas as they necessarily would to us.

That said, we don't know the inner wishes of the women involved. Especially when we talk about marriages, we are talking essentially about deals that are struck between men regarding the fate of women. And so we often find cases where people are put into marriage relationships where they may not want to be, but they feel like they have obligations to their family or they feel like they have no other choice, or not know any different.

Chairman ROYCE. I will just ask Mr. Watts if you observed the same thing in your interviews with these girls, and then I will follow that up, if I could, with another question.

Mr. WATTS. Yeah, I did. I met three women who had been essentially, as Dr. Ahram described, sold effectively to ISIS fighters through a deal with their family. ISIS targeted the poorest families. They were married to foreign fighters, all three of these girls, and in the process of indoctrination I think just is one of slow, day to day, as they described it to me. Literally slowly, slowly they began to persuade me about the force of their ideas. And I think that is one of the most important things to understand is that they are able to convince people that this is the correct way in which Islam is to be practiced, even women who don't agree.

Chairman ROYCE. Well, that was one of the points that Sasha had made in her written testimony. I didn't hear you say it here, but you had laid out this thesis that over time there had been sort of a movement of radicalization that, despite all the diversity around these continents, increasingly there was a new world view here being pushed. I don't know if that's in the Deobandi schools, or where it is. But this ideology, maybe you could articulate that, Sasha.

Ms. HAVLICEK. Yes. Absolutely. In my view, there has been an aggressive and very well-resourced, very well-funded export of a specific stream of thinking that is the intellectual underpinning for these movements, making it of course much easier in many senses to recruit to groups like ISIS.

Thirty years of export I have seen directly in regions like the Balkans where this Wahhabi Salafi ideology is absolutely alien to the local cultural traditions and practices of Islam. And they were sown insidiously in the aftermath of the war, when there was enormous desperation, economic and other, and Saudi charities setting up shop, providing handouts to families if they are—if they were to adopt stricter pre-modern Islamic codes.

This was done to some extent tongue in cheek by communities. It seemed sort of unimportant at the time, but it has had an absolutely insidious effect over the last 20 years and has shifted cultural norms. We really desperately need to be upholding those groups and individuals who usually with next to no support are trying to protect the very diverse cultural heritage and the practices of Islam in places of course as diverse, you know, as South Asia to the Balkans.

Chairman ROYCE. Do you see a role for mothers here? Because I can just tell you in West Africa, North Africa, Central Asia, I have heard this argument over and over and over again that they are changing our culture, they are changing my culture, from parents about what is happening to their children. And this has been going on now for maybe 20 years. I am trying to remember the first time I have heard it, but I have heard it so many times in so many communities.

Ms. HAVLICEK. I mean, women, as the primary vectors of cultural and religious transmission, are extremely important for extremists. Since well before ISIS, extremist organizations had propaganda targeting women. They know that if they have got women in their camp, the extremist project is much more likely to succeed, and so the cultural shifts will come through those women.

And so to some extent the shifts, as you have said, have been decades long, decades in the making. And so ISIS, in my view, is a kind of cherry on the cake but not the cake.

Chairman ROYCE. Mr. Engel.

Thank you.

Mr. ENGEL. Thank you, Mr. Chairman.

Dr. Kuehnast, let me ask you this. In your work in countering violent extremism, I understand that your organization has completed several assessments on women's programming in both Iraq and Afghanistan. And correct me if I am wrong, you found three areas in need of focus, which is reaching out to rural women, not just those in urban areas, engaging religious leaders, and working with men and boys.

Can you tell us—first of all, am I correct in the way I describe it? And can you tell us why these areas you have been working on and working in are important in countering violent extremism?

Ms. KUEHNAST. Yes. Thank you very much for the question. First of all, these were assessments that we did both on our work with the U.S. Government on women's programming in Iraq and in Afghanistan, but also engaged Iraqi and Afghan women.

Key issues that they identified are that because so much of the populations—and this would be true in parts of Africa as well—live in rural regions, whatever is happening among perhaps elite, educated women in the urban areas is not necessarily the same world that rural women live in. The access to information, certainly television, other forms of ways to learn what is going on in the world, is very reduced, and their worlds are reduced and much more hierarchical in terms of their status in the family.

That is why they recommended that no women's programming should be done in isolation or in a silo without engaging the men in their lives—the fathers, the brothers, the sons—as I mentioned in my testimony, that it is very key to begin engaging with a full gendered perspective, since men are, too, gendered beings. And we see, and ISIS has mentioned in other testimonies here today, that the concept of what it means to be a real man is being used very strategically, by women, by men, to influence young men. And so, again, it is important to bring men into this picture.

And, finally, of course, there are religious leaders, who for the most part in our world today are men. We must engage them in—certainly, in their perspectives on the role of women, both in the home and in public life, and also in the role that they can play in preventing violence.

I did want to comment just very briefly on the Soviet-Central Asia space, particularly in Kyrgyzstan. A year ago, we did a session with young university students in Kyrgyzstan, and they identified this issue of violent extremism, which they felt was growing, especially in the south of their country. It was related to the fact that for 70 years they were a secular country. They knew nothing about what Islam was. And, indeed, the very first propaganda, if you will, was the Wahhabis, who entered into South Central Asia.

And so part of the dilemma that they recommended to us was that we need to have much more engaged religious dialogue between religious experts on Islam and secular populations, so that people are understanding what is real Islam versus what is being promoted or propagated by extremist groups.

Thank you very much.

Mr. ENGEL. What have you found is the major difference between women in urban areas and women in rural areas? What have you found in your work that makes it harder for one group or another?

Ms. KUEHNAST. Very simply, time. Women living in rural regions often are having to access water, food, any kind of efforts on behalf of their children or parents, by foot. It is not like urban settings where there is transportation options available to them.

So time is of the essence, and the number of commitments that they have to make sure that there is food, that there is care for children and elderly, all of that very much limits their bandwidth in an everyday world. Radio is the best access, and we have found great success in our programs in South Sudan, in Iraq, in Afghanistan, using radio as a way to help shape positive messages.

Mr. ENGEL. Thank you.

Let me quickly, Mr. Watts, ask you—we saw a little clip of your film. It seemed extraordinary to me. It seems to me that the Yazidi lawyer could be living in a comfortable place, a comfortable life somewhere else in the world, and yet he risks everything to save these women and these girls.

I would like you to tell us a little more about that. What do you think drives him to do this? And how can he inspire others to help? What is the Iraqi Government doing about the situation, the missions this lawyer undertakes? Can it be cheap? How much do they cost? And who is funding them?

Mr. WATTS. Yeah. Well, he is an extraordinary individual, because, as you say, he has taken this on pretty much individually. There are about six guys, six or seven guys, who are actually involved in trying to organize these rescues. And they have essentially come up with a methodology completely off their own back, gathering information from women who have returned, making contact with people inside ISIS territory who don't agree with their views, or who are willing to help the network for money, as you say.

So he is an extraordinary character. There aren't many people like him necessarily, and I think he is doing it simply because this atrocity is so devastating to his community. It is an extremely conservative community, the Yazidis, where honor is very important, men and women live very separate lives, and ISIS has crashed in and essentially really hit the foundation of their community and their future of their community, because a lot of young boys have also been taken and are now being indoctrinated in ISIS's ideas.

In terms of the support they are getting, the Kurdish region of government has set up an office for the affairs of kidnapped people, which does, in a slightly ad hoc way, provide funds toward these rescue missions. Sometimes those missions occur for free, because there are people inside ISIS territory who are so opposed to ISIS's ideas they are willing to do it for humanitarian reasons.

There are other people who are so impoverished by the blockade of ISIS territory they are willing to help. There was a shepherd that was—I knew about who for $100 guided something like 20 people through the mountains.

But the problem is, this is all, as Khalil himself described it to me, it is a DIY operation. And that is one of the messages that I am hoping to get across to all of you today, is that these guys are doing extraordinary work inside ISIS territory. And through their work, we learn a much more realistic picture about what it is actually like inside ISIS territory.

There are people opposed to their rule. It is a dictatorship, enforcing a certain system of rules on a local population. And I think that their efforts could be supported in that way, and their work is also potentially giving us important intelligence that could guide a broader strategy as well.

Chairman ROYCE. We will go to—thank you. We will go to Chris Smith of New Jersey.

Mr. SMITH. Thank you so very much, Mr. Chairman. And I want to thank all of you for bearing expert witness to this pervasive, systematic exploitation against women, this violence against women, and for your policy recommendations, which will be very, very helpful.

Let me ask you, first, Ms. Havlicek, in your testimony, you point out that there is a shifting terrorist landscape, understanding women not just as victims but as perpetrators of extremism.

And, as we all know, all around the world, in human trafficking, syndicates often use women as the leaders in the subjugation of their victims. And the level of violence and gross indifference to the plight of those victims often equals that of their male trafficking partners.

And I am wondering if you could tell us, is that what it is like— is that what it is—are they using these women, ISIS, the ones that are becoming radicalized in that regard?

Let me also ask, you said with regards to our response that we need to reach the at-risk people directly, and all of you have pretty much cited some of the ways that that can be done through social media, and the like. But I am just wondering, in the counter strategy, what role do elementary and secondary schools, particularly in the West, have to play to try to provide a defense there?

Mr. Watts, you have pointed out that non-Muslim women are enslaved and raped. And I am wondering, you say how Muslim women are also oppressed and treated extremely harshly. But are they also sold? And what happens when a Muslim woman speaks out in some way, tries to defend other women who don't happen to be Muslim? Is she then really selected out for extreme punishment?

Dr. Kuehnast, if I could ask you, you made an excellent point about the focus on children. You point out that in March of this year the London-based monitoring group, the Syrian Observatory for Human Rights, found that ISIS had recruited at least 400 children, and that is in 3 months, you know, from the beginning of the year to March. At least—I am not sure what the time period is.

And I am wondering, is this parallel to child soldiers of Joseph Kony, Charles Taylor, that we saw in Africa? And then you talked about how they are shipped off to camps. Is that boys and girls? And where are those camps? What do they look like? If you could maybe elaborate a bit on that.

And, Dr. Ahram, you mentioned that ISIS selectively cites Medieval Islamic jurists to justify treating people from these groups as spoils, essentially property, and that they are raped at will, and you go on. Maybe you could elaborate on those Medieval texts and who these scholars are, and jurists, and that would be very helpful to the committee. And anything you can provide additionally for the record on that would also I think be very helpful.

[The information referred to follows:]

WRITTEN RESPONSE RECEIVED FROM ARIEL AHRAM, PH.D. TO QUESTION ASKED
DURING THE HEARING BY THE HONORABLECHRISTOPHER H. SMITH

Thank you for your question.

I believe that ISIS offers mere theological window dressing to justify sexual
enslavement and other acts that are purely and basely political.

Different schools of Islamic law that emerged in the ninth and tenth centuries
distinguish between different types of war and prescribe different codes of conduct
according to the identity of the enemy. Muslims armies were supposed to offer Jews,
Christians, and other monotheists a choice of conversion to Islam or accepting
subordination and protection in return for the right to retain their religion. The
treatment of groups considered polytheist or apostate from Islam is much harsher. If
they do not convert or return to the fold, they are not entitled to protection. Their
property can be seized and their wives taken as slaves, known as sabī. Still, there is no
clear conclusion among religious scholars about who fits in the category of polytheist or
apostate. The late Professor Majid Khadduri of Johns Hopkins University, author of
War and Peace in the Law of Islam, one of the most important books on Islamic theories of
war, noted that "all jurists, perhaps without exception, assert that polytheism and Islam
cannot exist together; the polytheists, who enjoin other gods with Allah, must choose
between war or Islam. The definition of a polytheist, however, has not been precisely
given by any jurist." This is equally true for apostasy. There have been endless debates
about which groups are definitively in or out of bounds for Islam. There has been a
general default toward more inclusive and tolerant definitions. In the 1970s, for
instance, Musa Sadr, the leader of the Shi'is in Lebanon, recognized the Alawis, which
many considered a fringe syncretistic group that melded Islam with other religious
practices, as Shi'is. There are also ecumenical trends among modern Islamic
theologians, recognizing the legitimacy of both Sunni and Shi'ite religious doctrine.

Equally importantly, few political leaders have been willing or able to put the most
belligerent religious principles into practice. Under Muslim rule, Iraq and Syria have
been characterized by a mosaic of religious communities. This included Sunni and
Shi'ite Muslims, Jews, and Christians of various sects. Yezidis, Druze, Shabak, and the
aforementioned Alawis practice a mix of animistic, Christian, and Islamic traditions.
Sufism, or Muslim mysticism, involving the veneration of saints and pilgrimage to holy
shrines, was also pervasive. It was not unusual for members of different religious
communities to revere the same shrines or saints. This is not to say that there was
inter-communal harmony. However, mass violence was relatively rare.

ISIS's drive to annihilate Yezidis, Shabak, Alawis, and Shi'is appears justified by a
particular and idiosyncratic reading of Islamic law derived from the writings of Ibn
Taymiyya, an Islamic jurist who died in 1328. While hardly decisive in his own day, Ibn
Taymiyya's views were adopted by the jurist Muhammad ibn Abd al-Wahhab in the
eighteenth century and became the ideological foundation of the Kingdom of Saudi
Arabia. Ibn Taymiyya was also a major influence on Sayyed Qutb, an Egyptian

dissident activist who is widely considered to be intellectual fount for contemporary Islamic radicalism.

ISIS has an extremely narrow definition of what it means to be Muslim and, reciprocally, an expansive definition of polytheism and apostasy. They see groups like the Yezidis, Shabak, and Alawis as polytheistic or deviationists from true Islam. They are profoundly hostile to Shi'ism, which they see as apostasy. They deem the veneration of saints, pilgrimages, and other practices that are common to many religions in Syria and Iraq to be tantamount to idol-worship. ISIS takes it as an obligation to wage war against any and all groups that dispute their religious interpretations, regardless of whether these groups believe themselves to be Muslim.

But ISIS has been supremely self-serving and selective in interpreting even its own religious dogma. For example, ISIS has had very close operational collaboration with another Iraqi militant group called the Jaysh Rijal al-Tariq al-Naqshbandi (Army of the Men of the Naqshbandi Order). The Naqshbandi order is an ancient and well-established Muslim Sufi group in northern Iraq. Traditional Naqshbandi practices include veneration of saints and pilgrimages, placing them among the idolaters by Ibn Taymiyya's criteria. JRTN emerged in 2006 under the leadership of Izzat Ibrahim al-Duri, one Saddam Husayn's top lieutenants and also a sheikh, or mystical guide, of the order. JRTN was composed most of ex-Ba'thists like Duri. Despite the fact that JRTN's religious rituals are anathema to ISIS's interpretation of Islam, this did not prevent a close working relationship between the two groups. In fact, JRTN was instrumental in helping ISIS infiltrate and seize Mosul in 2014. This alliance is illustrative of how military and political necessities override religious injunctions for ISIS.

Treating captured Yezidis and Shabak women as spoils and slaves is similarly a political act. More than anything in the Quran or medieval Islamic history, ISIS's abuse of Yezidis and Shabak bears many similarities to the genocidal Anfal campaign. Like ISIS today, Saddam's government used rape as part of its campaign of ethnic cleansing against Kurds in the late 1980s. Considering the close relationship between ISIS and the former Iraqi Ba'th party officials, it is probable that ISIS models its violent practices on these more recent and immediate experiences. Additionally, ISIS's use of rape mirrors the campaign of sexual violence waged by the Syrian government especially against suspected rebel sympathizers. This again, provides a likely model for action and motive for revenge. Please see my article "Sexual Violence in the Making of ISIS" in *Survival* (Vol. 53, No. 3, 2015) for further details. In summary, sexual violence is less a religious imperative than a means to reward fighters, generate revenue, and solidify a new political order.

Mr. SMITH. Ms. Havlicek.
Ms. HAVLICEK. Thank you so much. In terms of the first question about how they are being used, I think it is very clear that ISIS has had a targeted strategy to recruit women, so they value them as part of the operation on a number of different fronts.
They are using Western women in particular in the propaganda recruitment machinery that they have developed so successfully. Western women are prolific in social media spaces. They are providing both practical advice to women and men as to how to get out there, how to avoid security services, their parents, and so on, and then of course ideological advice and propagandizing.
They are very important from a PR perspective, because the fact of a young Western woman leaving all of the so-called freedoms of the Western world and choosing of her own volition to travel to ISIS territory and to adopt this new life and world, is extremely

compelling. And, of course, the PR value is also in the fact that media has disproportionately covered this story of Western girls, so they know that they are high PR value.

The piece of this which is really troop morale strategy is about making sure that fighters, foreign fighters writ large, who like the idea of Western brides are getting a steady stream of these girls in. There is a functional dimension to this.

And then, of course, the question of building the next generation. That is I think key. They are taking a long-term view on the life of ISIS. This is the state-building piece of the strategy, which is really about rearing the next generation of jihadis. And so in so many ways that radicalization is absolutely intrinsic for the success of the long-term project.

On the second point, you asked about what we could be doing in schools for instance. I think that there is an absolutely critical job to be done on inoculating young people in two ways. One, we need a much, much better, a stronger approach to sensitizing young people to extremist propaganda. And we need critical thinking skills specifically in terms of how young people are using the internet.

We have developed a program which combines extremely—and I should say, you know, myth-busting doesn't work for young people in this space. What is drawing them in is the incredibly emotive material that they are being exposed to on a 24/7 basis in these social media environments, in the echo chambers that they are entering into online. It is extremely emotive.

And so we can't come back with a set of facts about what doesn't work. We need emotive stories to counter that, the sort of work that Mr. Watts has done, absolutely critical. But, again, the voices of formers, of survivors, are absolutely critical.

We have developed a series of films based on those sorts of testimonies, and accompanied that with a state-of-the-art tool for teachers, a set of guides for teachers to use that kind of material interactively in a school setting, in a community center setting, for parents to start to engage their children in the difficult conversations that need to be had now with young people about what they are starting to see or about to start to see. They need to be inoculated.

Chairman ROYCE. Ms. Havlicek, we best go to Albio Sires of New Jersey. Thanks.

Mr. SIRES. Thank you, Mr. Chairman, for holding this hearing, and thank you for being here.

Mr. Watts, that is pretty powerful in just a few minutes. I am just wondering when these survivors—or when you reunite some of these children and women, how damaged are they? Do they make it back? I mean——

Mr. WATTS. The damage is incredibly severe. It is the worst I have seen, having covered conflicts and sexual violence in a number of places around the world. If you see the film, there is one example of a 21-year-old girl who suffered a physical traumatic flashback as she was describing what she had been through, where she physically struggled for breath, she collapsed, she effectively passed out and had to be brought around with medical assistance. And her case is not isolated.

I spoke to a doctor who is dealing with the women coming back who said that that was actually quite a common phenomenon. I think partly because of these girls—they are very young, they are from a conservative society that has had no real education about sex, and then they are taken into the worst possible sexual atrocities imaginable, and the effect on their mind is quite severe.

Physically, though, as well, there was a case of a 9-year-old girl. I didn't meet her myself. She had been raped multiple times and was now pregnant. And, you know, it is really the most extreme physical and psychological trauma that you can imagine, and they are pretty understaffed as well to handle it.

Mr. SIRES. Do they have any kind of normal life after this? Not just you; anybody else that wants to. Doctor?

Mr. WATTS. Well, I would say that I—I met an 18-year-old girl who had been raped. During her testimony to me, she described being gang-raped on two occasions and raped in total by up to 30 different fighters. And she is 18. I met her for dinner the other day to give her her first pizza. And if you saw her in the street, you would not believe what happened to her. She seemed like a normal 18-year-old girl, laughing, joking.

So I believe that these young women and girls have such incredible strength. They show amazing powers of recovery. But it is incredibly difficult to overcome what they have been through.

Mr. SIRES. I find that hard to believe, but I take your word for it.

Ms. KUEHNAST. Thank you. I would just add a couple of thoughts here. There are neurologists and neuroscientists who are studying the impact of extreme trauma on the human brain. And I think that is why in my testimony I am advocating for more data. We know that it affects literally the brain, and that is why this type of trauma happening to a child could affect them the rest of their lives.

There is no doubt, though, that one of the other major findings that we are seeing is that the vulnerability of this next generation as a result of trauma sets us up for more concerns. There is a phenomenal researcher, Dr. Wendy Lower, who studied the role of women in the Nazi killing fields. And one of her premises is, what happened in World War I, and what they witnessed, helped set up the situation and the vulnerability for the engagement of women and children in these efforts. We should learn from our history as well.

Mr. SIRES. You know, Muslim scholars and imams from around the world have called ISIL members un-Islamic and have condemned the treatment of women they have captured. Some believe that the battle against ISIS can be won by winning the hearts and minds of these fighters through transforming their view of women as part of the Islam faith. Would you agree with that assessment? Doctor?

Mr. AHRAM. I think this relates both to your question and to Congressman Smith, and I will have to offer commitments for the record in more detail.

Mr. SIRES. Doctor, would you just hit that button there?

Mr. AHRAM. I will have to offer comments for the record in more detail. But I think that one of the most important things about ISIS is that they have looked at Islamic history through a lens really fashioned by a thinker, an Egyptian thinker named Sayyid

Qutb offered the idea that in certain circumstances Muslims were in a position to declare other Muslims to be apostate, to be un-Islamic. That was really an innovation that came about in the 1940s and 1950s.

That ability to say that "We are real Muslims and you are not," had never really existed in the Islamic world before. ISIS is very aggressive in declaring that other groups that consider themselves to be Muslim, that they are not legitimate. And because they are not legitimate, they can be targeted.

So I think that it really is a battle of ideas within the Muslim world, just as much as it is a competition between what Dr. Havlicek described as a battle between the West and the Islamic world. There very much is a great deal of contention about who has the right to determine what is Islamically permissible.

Mr. SIRES. Thank you very much.

Chairman ROYCE. Thank you.

Mr. Jeff Duncan of South Carolina. Will pass.

Mr. Ted Yoho of Florida.

Mr. YOHO. Thank you, Mr. Chairman, and I appreciate your testimonies here. If you guys could kind of give me the outline of a person, what makes a person want to go over there from a Western culture? What is the demographics you see? Age? Financial background? Religious background? Family structure, if you have that, that would draw somebody to that? I just—I find it unfathomable that somebody would do that by choice.

Ms. HAVLICEK. Perhaps I could take that up. Based on the dataset that we have just of Western women joining ISIS, what is interesting is that they don't lend themselves easily to profiling, to actionable profiling. They are very diverse in terms of their socioeconomic backgrounds, in terms even of their religious backgrounds, and in terms of their educational attainment. We do see girls, in general, more educated than boys, some as educated as doctors.

Mr. YOHO. Let me interrupt you here. Have you done retrospective studies going backwards, after you have found people over there that have gone over there, and then gone back and say, "All right. You came from this background; you have done that"?

Ms. HAVLICEK. That is right. We are looking at the backgrounds of the girls and women in our dataset who have migrated from Western countries and are now living in ISIS territory, as far as we can see it from the data.

And there are some trends. We are seeing on average the age diminishing in terms of female recruits in line with the fact that of course the fighters will want untarnished wives, obviously unmarried girls. We are seeing—we do see a high proportion of converts within that group, and I think that that is coming across radicalization, women and men. But essentially they are not lending themselves to that kind of social profiling.

In terms of the—what has been interesting is looking at the narratives that they themselves use to justify their own departures from the West, their own joining of ISIS. There is a number of narratives that are quite prevalent, some of which are common to the male datasets that we look at.

They are about the global Muslim community being under attack, about the inaction of the international community to do anything about that, about their own feelings of isolation within Western societies, and then—and as I mentioned, for the girls, there is a gendered aspect of that identity questioning, which is really about whether the Western emancipation project has resulted in what we thought it would.

Does it in fact free, or does it enslave you in some other way? And so the narrative is actually about getting away from the "tyranny" of Western female emancipation to some extent as part of that narrative, and justifies the extremely puritanical iterations that we see of Islam.

Mr. YOHO. All right. Let me ask Dr. Kuehna—is it Kuehnast?

Ms. KUEHNAST. Kuehnast.

Mr. YOHO. Kuehnast. What are you finding? Are the women that are going over there, are they from an indigenous culture, born here in a Western society, in Europe? Or are they from a Middle Eastern background that has migrated there? Maybe first generation or second generation, and there is a draw on them bringing them back to that area.

Ms. KUEHNAST. I would defer to my colleague, who probably has the data——

Mr. YOHO. That is fine.

Ms. KUEHNAST [continuing]. Set more. But I will speak as a Central Asianist and what I know about that region. There are families actually going, so it is not even—they are going in groups. And some of the motivation is the draw of the income, especially as the labor migrants to Russia has narrowed, and so we see a push factor there that is often not necessarily ideological but an opportunity, if you will, to work.

Mr. YOHO. What country do we see most of them coming from? Is there one specifically? Is it all over the European area?

Ms. KUEHNAST. Tunisia.

Mr. YOHO. Tunisia?

Ms. KUEHNAST. Right?

Mr. YOHO. Is that what you are seeing, too?

Ms. HAVLICEK. Yes. I mean, from across Western countries, it is—again, it is very, very diverse. Ethnically speaking, the group is extremely diverse. In terms of our data, it is very, very poor with regards to recruitment from countries in the region, and that is one of the challenges that we do see.

It is absolutely true that in a Western context what we are seeing, and certainly since the announcement of the caliphate, we tend to see girls going solo, unmarried women and girls going solo or in small groups.

Mr. YOHO. I am out of time, and I appreciate your questions—or your answers, and I appreciate the work you are all doing. Thank you.

I yield back.

Chairman ROYCE. Thank you. We will go to Brad Sherman of California.

Mr. SHERMAN. Thank you, Mr. Chairman. I am glad we are having a series of hearings on women. There is a tremendous correlation between a society's development and the opportunities for women. The more women are given a chance to expand their horizons, the richer, the more advanced the society becomes. And the more advanced the society becomes, the more women are included in it.

We may disagree on some elements of family planning and some other things that I would like to see as part of international women's agenda, but I think our overlap would be quite substantial.

This hearing is also about ISIS, and I think we have got to remember the enemies of ISIS are more dangerous and more evil than ISIS. Turkey believes that perhaps in the wrong way. They are bombing ISIS. They are bombing Kurdish groups that are fighting ISIS. If you look at Syria where the Shiite alliance has killed 200,000 people, we can say that is not as evil as ISIS because they don't put the exploding bodies on YouTube. They do not show the gruesomeness. They do not delight in the gruesomeness. But they killed 200,000 people, and those deaths are every bit as painful. They are just not on YouTube.

The Shiite alliance in Iran where they are developing nuclear weapons, obviously, the Shiite militias that dominate the political scene in southern Iraq, Hezbollah, and of course Assad, should remind us that whatever we do against ISIS it cannot be for the benefit of the Shiite alliance.

I have spent some time in this room talking about how our State Department can't possibly respond to the ideological threat of ISIS, because they refuse to hire anyone on the basis of their understanding of Islamic law, history, and jurisprudence. They won't hire anybody who doesn't have a certain number of Western academic brownie points.

Now, you can be close to the top of your class at Princeton, or you can be the valedictorian at Cal State University at Northridge. But if you are just an Islamic scholar, and that is the only thing on your resume, you will not be hired. So what does this mean? It means we are fumbling around in the dark.

We might show pictures of how gruesome and terrible it is that Yazidi girls are being forced to convert. But I don't know whether someone who accepts the tenets of the most extreme versions of Islam regards that as a terrible act or a wonderful way to help this woman, because I am not an Islamic scholar, let alone a scholar of extremist Islam.

And I am not saying the State Department should issue fatwas, but we are doing a lot of unsigned advertising on the internet, designed to appeal to folks who have an extremist and deep motivating connection with Islam, and nobody writing these ads has much knowledge of Islam.

And we occasionally might go to Islamic jurists and ask them the issue of fatwa, but it would be like writing a brief for an American judge saying, ''Please issue a ruling. And I am writing this to you, but I am not a lawyer and I haven't cited any cases. But the truth of my—the justice of my comments are so overwhelming.''

Nobody would try to get an American judge to issue a ruling without hiring a lawyer and convincing that judge not on the basis of righteous compassion, but also on the basis of the things that lawyers and judges do.

Dr. Ahram, you say that it wasn't until like the 1940s that the concept of apostasy was known in Islam. And I had thought that the Alawites and the Ahmadis had been accused of being apostates long before that. I mean, you have got, in the case of the Alawites, people who drink alcohol. You are saying until the '40s nobody called them apostates?

Mr. AHRAM. They had been called apostates, but the primary consensus had been that since no one was really in a position to be sure what "apostasy" means that no one should really be in a position to take action based on that consideration.

ISIS, and other groups, have decided that they are in a position not only to be the judge but also the executioner when it comes to these decisions. They can make a decision about who is apostate and to carry out the sentence for apostasy.

Mr. SHERMAN. Ms. Havlicek, what portion of the Western women who are going to join ISIS have parents who are Muslims, and what portion of them are folks with non-Muslim parents who first converted to Islam and then decided to join ISIS? Any guess?

Ms. HAVLICEK. Obviously, ISIS is recruiting among young Muslims, so it is, in fact, the majority are Muslims. But there is a——

Mr. SHERMAN. Well, there are two ways to be—two histories——

Ms. HAVLICEK. Right.

Mr. SHERMAN [continuing]. Of people who become Muslim, those who convert and those who are born.

Ms. HAVLICEK. Yeah. So the conversion rate is very high per capita, within the dataset that we have, in that——

Mr. SHERMAN. So a significant number of the women going have non-Muslim parents, were not born Muslim, they converted to Islam, then in fact converted to extremist Islam, and then converted to ISIS.

Ms. HAVLICEK. That is right.

Mr. SHERMAN. Yield back.

Chairman ROYCE. We need to go to David Trott of Michigan.

Mr. TROTT. Thank you, Mr. Chairman. I also want to thank the ranking member for scheduling this hearing, and I want to thank all of the witnesses today for coming and sharing your insight. It is pretty clear from your comments we are not dealing with the JV team, and it is a little frustrating because, you know, sitting here listening to the discussion of the various atrocities, that is certainly productive because it draws attention to the problem and that needs to happen.

But I can't help but feel that either because of a lack of understanding, or a general insouciance, that we don't have a plan. And so my comments—you know, my questions really shift more from discussing the problem, which all of you will have a better understanding of the problem than perhaps anyone in Congress ever will.

So, to that end, I want to ask the entire panel, each of you, if you could give me a couple ideas, a couple solutions. And my question is two-fold. First, I would like you each to speak to how you feel the State Department's response to this problem has been.

And then, beyond that, specifically, if you each could offer a couple ideas of things that Congress could work on or Congress could focus on or Congress could ask the administration to work on, what you think the resources and implementation would be required. It would be particularly helpful if the ideas don't require a lot of money, because we don't have a lot of extra tax dollars sitting around.

But whatever your—if you were in charge for a day, what are the two things you would do in Congress or in the administration to make a difference on these issues? And we will start with you, Ms. Havlicek.

Ms. HAVLICEK. Thank you so much. We understand that $26 billion has been spent to date on training the Iraqi army over the last decade. I mention that figure because in the United Kingdom this last year we allocated 40 million pounds to the prevention side of this problem, that is to say, in a way the soft power side of this problem.

I don't think it is serious. There is a quote of Osama Bin Laden of 2002 that says,

> "It is obvious that the media war in this century is one of the strongest methods. In fact, its ratio may reach 90 percent of the total preparation for battles."

We have not taken on this soft power piece of the battle in a serious way. It, of course, does not require the type of funding that the hard power piece of this battle requires, by any stretch of the imagination, it will be an enormous amount cheaper.

But just very quickly, I don't believe that a soft power strategy can be delivered just through government counter messaging centers. I don't, in fact, believe that counter narrative can be delivered by government. It has to be developed by credible voices. We have talked about a few of those constituencies here.

Networks also of women are important in this, but former extremists, survivors of extremism, are important, credible voices. But those voices tend not to have the tools, the skills to be able to get their messages out at scale in any sustained way or in any strategic way. They have not been empowered. We need the power of our communications and tech sector on side to do that at scale, and that needs to be a combination things. So that has not happened as yet.

We desperately need to do the intellectual challenging of "Brand Caliphate," and to do that we need to be building the sorts of networks, really working with the sorts of people that Mr. Watts is working with to get those ideas and stories out in a much, much bigger way.

I do think that one of the things—one of the problems has been that governments, by and large, have focused essentially on this challenge of propaganda through regulatory response. That is to say, we want to take that nasty stuff down. That Whac-A-Mole approach tends in fact not to work. We have now just seen the establishment of a Europole Referral Center, which is to say lots of people in a room flagging nasty material and hoping that the internet companies will take it down. That happens very slowly.

When accounts are taken down, of course, they go up very fast, but our research has shown interestingly that the second accounts of women, for instance, prolific recruiters and radicalizers, the second accounts of those women, once their first accounts have been taken down, tend to be more influential, i.e. more followers.

And so we have to be careful that we are not doing counterproductive things in the takedown space, and so I would very much propose that we focus instead in a much, much more serious way on the counter narrative. I do believe that that needs to be mainstreamed in government policymaking through aid and diplomatic efforts.

If we were to combine those efforts and those budgets, we would finally have the muscle in place to do something in this space. It does require that extremism, not just the violent piece of extremism, the non-violent piece of extremism that lays the intellectual foundations for extremism, is taken seriously and mainstreamed across policymaking centers.

Chairman ROYCE. Mr. Gerry Connolly of Virginia.

Mr. CONNOLLY. Thank you, Mr. Chairman.

Just picking up on what you just said, Ms. Havlicek, it seems to me that if it is going to be efficacious that needs to be an Islamic message, not a Western message.

Ms. HAVLICEK. Absolutely. I am sorry if that wasn't clear.

Mr. CONNOLLY. No, no. I wasn't correcting you. I am just observing based on what you——

Ms. HAVLICEK. Well, and credible voices as a whole are of course voices from within the communities, and they can be very diverse voices——

Mr. CONNOLLY. Yes.

Ms. HAVLICEK [continuing]. From within the communities. And when I talk about building the networks, I mean networks of those front-line voices.

Mr. CONNOLLY. I understand. I am just so horrified, frankly, at the details of this hearing. For me, it starts with the whole issue of human autonomy. It is easy to compromise someone else's autonomy when I objectify them as apostate or "the other." By the way, not at all an Islamic phenomenon. I mean, that kind of objectifying of human beings has been going on since human beings arrived on the planet.

I mean, there is a long, sad, tragic Christian tradition of doing that, Turquemada to wit. Heretics could be burned, because they were in error, although it seems to me that there is a contradiction here in this behavior with the Koran itself. And I would be interested in your observations.

I also find it ironic that we are recruiting with 21st century Western social media. We are recruiting foot soldiers for a ninth century caliphate. And I just wonder if the cruel irony of that has struck anybody in the region.

And then, finally, susceptibility, and I particularly would like your reaction to that, although the other two as well. It is very hard for us I think culturally to understand, outside of brainwashing, how can somebody—how can a culture, how can a village, how can large numbers of people being recruited elsewhere be so susceptible to such a barbaric, suppressive message and culture, whether you are a female or male.

And what does that mean for us going forward as we try to think about a stable future some day? I know these are broad questions, but I think we need to better understand the susceptibility here, and some of it may very well have to do with, frankly, in some cultures the willingness to suppress women.

Not like ISIS, but the sort of second-class for women, clearly not the equal of male, that culture ISIS is preying upon. I mean, it is taking it to an absurd degree, but—and I just wondered what your observations are about that, because I think if we are going to counter it we need to know a lot more than we know right now. Anyone?

Ms. KUEHNAST. Well, I just want to reinforce what you are asking in this fact that, indeed, I don't think this is anything new to the human race. It is just we do now have YouTube and photos and videos that document these atrocities. And in that fact it is new and it is what you say. We are seeing the impact of 21st century technology that we thought was about freedom of expression, about autonomy being used as a tool for extreme propaganda and violence.

So, indeed, it is ironic, and it is troubling. But it is not necessarily a regulation issue. It is—we have been at this juncture as a human race before in moments of great technological shift. And we know we can also address it.

Your comments about women and their role in society, there is a professor at Texas A&M, Valerie Hudson, who is basically working on a project, called Women Stats, where very convincing evidence is showing that those states that have gender equality, the chances for violence and conflict are much lower; that it is correlated, statistically speaking.

Chairman ROYCE. We will go to Ileana Ros-Lehtinen from Florida.

Ms. ROS-LEHTINEN. Thank you so much, Mr. Chairman. Thank you for convening this important hearing on a crucial subject that is often overlooked. I regret that I have to get back to the floor. I would like my statement to be made a part of the record.

Chairman ROYCE. Without objection.

Ms. ROS-LEHTINEN. But I am pleased to yield my time to Chris Smith, so that Congressman Smith can get the answers about the camps.

Thank you.

Chairman ROYCE. The gentleman is recognized.

Mr. SMITH. Thank you very much. I thank my good friend for yielding.

You know, you just mentioned, Doctor, Valerie Hudson. I actually had Valerie Hudson testify at a hearing that I held on the consequences of gendercide in China. She wrote the unbelievably ground-breaking book, "Bare Branches," about what sex election abortion has done to China, and the missing daughters who have been at 5 months or so gestation, as babies, forcibly aborted.

They are only allowed one, so they choose the male, and the impact it is having on an increasingly male and older society, and China is in a terrible, terrible demographic meltdown that could lead to violence. She even said—Valerie Hudson—that it could lead to war because of the missing females in that country, again underscoring the need for—and the absolutely indispensable role that we all know—we take it for granted here—that women play in society.

But when they are missing and they are dead, then that is not the case. But Valerie Hudson is an extraordinary academic and writer.

Let me just ask—I had asked those earlier questions to you about the tiny terrorists that you talked about, the child soldiers maybe is another way of putting it, how any of that compares with the LRA or Charles Taylor. The camps I don't have a sense—I don't think any of us perhaps do—what those camps really look like. And let me—and you did compare it to the Hitler Youth, which certainly is a staggering comparison.

Mr. Watts, again, if you could get to the issue of the women who might step up and help another woman who is—Muslim helps a non-Muslim, what happens to her.

You also talked about the brainwashing. If any of you could speak to what is being done for any child or person who needs to go through the deprogramming of the hate. In Africa, obviously, there are a number of programs for child soldiers that do work, not perfectly, but I have met many of them. We have had them here testifying.

Lastly, before I run out of time again, for the second time, if I could just ask about, Dr. Ahram, on the Medievals. And if you could provide that for the record, we all want to read that, and I thank you for your answer, if you could elaborate on that, please.

Ms. KUEHNAST. I will just basically say, in terms of this relevant information with the LRA and Uganda with Joseph Kony, absolutely, I think, you know, the Lost Boys, we see that. But I think what is different, if you will, is Joseph Kony, as a renegade armed actor in a war, certainly did not have the advantage of YouTube.

And I do think that that is, as our colleagues here have so well put, the PR value of making these video clips of little boys carrying guns that are bigger than them, any of these visualizations have enormous emotional impact, as Sasha mentioned earlier.

I would add South Sudan to this mix, because we know for a fact that the number of children being kidnapped, both boys and girls, to be armed actors in this civil conflict is rising, and the use of sexual violence there is really tipping the charts. So ISIS is not the only actor here who has figured out that sexual violence is cheaper than a bullet. And it is so much more effective; it is terror at its deepest level. And it does destroy people, and it destroys the ties that bond people together.

And when you have to witness a child being raped, a mother being raped, as many of these things are public spectacles, then you are on the edge of what we call in the genocide prevention work, on the edge of an atrocity, a human atrocity. This is one of the key indicators of genocidal behavior is gang rape.

Mr. SMITH. The camps—because I am running out of time again—the camps, what do they look like, and where are they?

Ms. KUEHNAST. What we see on the videos and photos and YouTubes, they are basic. They are very basic, but they give them an identity, a uniform, a gun, and they practice, as I mentioned, cutting off first doll heads, so that they are prepared to do the next.

And as Dr. Ahram said, sexual violence among—against boys is very high. Very, very high, because it creates shame and it creates belonging in an ironic manner.

Chairman ROYCE. Well, we had better go to Lois Frankel now. But perhaps when we get back at the end of some of the questioning, maybe by Judge Poe, we can get to that.

Thank you.

Ms. FRANKEL. Thank you, Mr. Chair. And thank you for this hearing, and thank you to the panel. I will—I am like everybody else sitting here. This is just an appalling situation, and to me you have just been describing the lowest form of humanity. And I am not sure what we can do. I am going to—I want to follow up on Mr. Trott's questions, but I know one thing. We cannot turn our back on this.

Mr. Trott asked you for some examples—or some concrete suggestions, and I think, Ms. Havlicek, you have had—I know you gave us your ideas. I would like to hear the ideas from some of you. And if you could just also take into account—you know, you said there were 4 million women living under ISIS control or contested areas.

So, obviously, there are a lot of these areas, they are war zones, so I am not sure—how do you infiltrate these areas? And, you know, what are the—I think you talked about the radio, the internet. I don't know. Are we talking about NGOs, civil society? Could you give us some really concrete examples?

Mr. WATTS. I think there is a very specific example, and it is one of the things I was going to say in answer to Mr. Trott's question, which is we need to remember the lessons of previously when America was directly engaged against al-Qaeda in Iraq, as it was called then, which was the awakening which did so much to end their reign of terror then was based on personal relationships, on a particular Sunni tribal sheikh who walked into the American base at the end of his road and said, ''I know where these guys are hiding. I know where they keep their guns.'' And from that point on, in a matter of days, he was able to—they were able to transform the military situation.

And what I am saying is that the network that I came across in the Yazidi territory that also exists in parts of Syria, there are people on the ground. There is a huge, I think, population. Some of the people out there say to me 60 percent of the population in ISIS territory are opposed to them. There are assassinations that these groups carry out against ISIS members of their own volition.

If we can just expand on the contacts that already exist, build up the personal relationships, follow the line of the network, then perhaps we can begin to make contact with people inside who oppose ISIS's views and are in a position to help direct our efforts, you know, whether they have been military or humanitarian, better.

And I think that is my second point in answer to Mr. Trott's. He asked for two things, which is that if we are going to do something we should do it right, like the air strikes are happening, and I get an email every day reporting what has been destroyed.

But on the front line, I was with Kurdish fighters, and we saw trucks passing within 100 meters on the highway between Mosul and Al-Hasakah and Raqqah. And I said, ''What is going on with these trucks?'' And they said, ''We don't have any spotters that are authorized to call in strikes on this stuff.'' So I think that small steps can be taken that would just make the effort more effective.

Ms. KUEHNAST. I mentioned in my comments that refugee camps are there. They have information. They know about what is going. They have fleed, and they have opportunities now, one, to try to heal from what they have seen and experienced, and we should be right there, because this will be the next generation if we don't engage them.

We can't leave them to be idle, because the opportunity to intersect with idleness and the opportunity for engaging in the extremist efforts are provocative because they provide money, identity, and opportunity. So refugee camps are key, focusing on young people, very young people, under 10.

We just should take the playbook from ISIS. They are focusing on young people. Why aren't we? And in the same light, we need to pay attention to what Edward said here. Focus on the relationships. They are doing it one person at a time. They don't have this massive campaign. They do it one person at a time, and they spend a lot of time on just one. Individuals count. In the same way, we need to make those networks and relationships matter.

Mr. AHRAM. There are, at present, 36 different local and international NGOs and U.S. agencies involved specifically on gender violence in Lebanon, Syria, Jordan, Turkey, and Iraq. I think those would be the agencies that have the most direct access to victims and are in a position to try and assist their reintegration back into society.

I think also, though, it is worth cautioning about the impact of military intervention. Military interventions are going to produce more population displacement, and population displacement, people who are displaced—and there are already 13 million displaced people in Syria and Iraq today. Those are the people that are most vulnerable to all kinds of sexual trafficking, to sexual exploitation and to rape.

And so I think that while there is certainly a purpose in destroying ISIS, I would caution that there will be a humanitarian blowback as well, and there will be humanitarian costs to those kinds of activities.

Chairman ROYCE. We will go to Judge Ted Poe of Texas.

Mr. POE. Thank you, Mr. Chairman. Thank you all for being here.

I want to center in on specifically the issue of women being trafficked by ISIS, human trafficking. Do we have any estimates about how much money is made by ISIS in the trafficking of women and girls? Does anybody know?

Ms. KUEHNAST. I was just going to say this is an absolutely important point, to see that this is a huge criminal network. It is very entrepreneurial, and it is making a lot of money. The numbers——

Mr. POE. Does anybody know how much money? Any estimate at all?

Mr. WATTS. I don't have an estimate on the exact figure, but the trafficking is primarily within—when we are talking about sex slaves, for example, the women and girls from the Yazidi community, it is within ISIS. So——

Mr. POE. Right. How many women are we talking about there would be in trafficking?

Mr. WATTS. In terms of the sex, there——

Mr. POE. Sex trafficking, yes.

Mr. WATTS. Sex slaves, it is over 3,000, is what we think.

Mr. POE. How does ISIS justify sex trafficking?

Mr. WATTS. By its definition of this particular religious minority, the Yazidis. Specifically, they are the only group that we know for certain have been——

Mr. POE. Tell me how they justify it. They do justify it, I agree. How do they justify it?

Mr. WATTS. They say they are pagans, and they judge them by the treatment of pagans back in the—1,300 years ago.

Mr. POE. And a pagan is what?

Mr. WATTS. A pagan is someone who——

Mr. POE. In their eyes, under their definition.

Mr. WATTS. Like an animist, basically, someone who worships rocks or animals or, you know, sees gods all over the place, sees a multitude of gods. The Yazidis, for example, they use the sun. They are actually monotheistic, so actually ISIS have got their interpretation of the Yazidi religion wrong, but the Yazidis view the sun or they use the sun as a particular symbol to symbolize God.

And in ISIS's interpretation, that means that they are worshiping something other than Allah, a clear—you know, an animist symbol.

Mr. POE. Then that would include everybody that doesn't agree with their specific religious doctrine. Is that correct or not?

Mr. WATTS. That is not correct in the sense that the Koran does have certain outlines for the treatment of the people of the book, i.e. Christians and Jews. And so there aren't—you know, it doesn't apply to everybody.

Mr. POE. Well, does it apply to Jews and Christians?

Mr. WATTS. It doesn't, as far as we know, as far as—to the best of my knowledge. Though Christians have been abducted, they haven't been subjected to this kind of sexual enslavement as the Yazidis have. That is the only group, to the best of my knowledge, that has been treated in that way.

Mr. POE. But none of you have any numbers, any kind of numbers that we are talking about?

Mr. WATTS. Well, we are talking about over 3,000, as I say, women and girls. And the price for a girl, if she is a virgin, can be up to $2,000, I heard in testimony. But after she has been subjected to multiple sexual assaults, the price can go down to as low as $100 to $50.

And what is happening is that girls are being—one girl literally described it to me. She was rented out. So she would be passed around for 50 bucks here, 100 bucks there, and so—but, again, that money is all being transmitted internally within ISIS. To the best of our knowledge, they are not trafficking outside their boundaries.

Mr. POE. I understand.

Ms. Havlicek, let me ask you something about countering violent extremism. We have a program, supposedly, through the State Department to counter violent extremism. This is just my opinion. We are—it seems we are losing that battle with countering violent extremism and the results.

Can you weigh in on that issue, U.S. countering violent extremism, as it deals with sex trafficking of women? Would you like to weigh in on that?

Ms. HAVLICEK. I am not in a position to speak about the sex trafficking piece of that question. But if I might just respond on the U.S. CVE structure.

Mr. POE. Sure.

Ms. HAVLICEK. I do think that we have tended to view this battle in a slightly narrow way. The idea that you are going to beat this enormous propaganda recruitment machinery, this movement through a sort of hashtag war, is just too narrow a perspective.

As I mentioned earlier, I don't think that counter messaging can be done—counter narrative work can credibly be done if led by government. I think governments have a job to do on their own strategic communications. No question. But during the Cold War, there was a serious investment in the battle of ideas, an investment that understood the need to build civil society networks in all sorts of different ways through educational outreach, through NGOs, and in so many different ways.

And those were the people, of course, that were at the front line of the transition processes when, in fact, there was an opportunity to see that happen. That kind of investment I think has not happened in this particular case, and I would hope we could. I think one of the problems is that we are also always seeing governments running after the fact.

We are responsive and certainly not proactive. I would make a plea for us to look at the displaced populations. The refugee situation, as you well know, it is the single largest humanitarian crisis of our time. We need, for both moral imperative reasons, and from a practical perspective, to be getting to grips with that population: 5 million, 6 million people, 4 million outside of the country.

That is going to be the pool from which extremists recruit. That is going to be our biggest challenge and threat over the next generation. We are seeing absolutely nothing being done in the prevention space on those communities and populations right now. That would be a way for us to get a little bit ahead of the curve. Also, we have said the same thing about women. Here is an emerging threat, a trend, that hasn't really been—that hasn't really gone up the food chain in terms of priorities for policymakers.

And I must say, though, that the State Department has been proactive in looking at ways in which to partner with civil society organizations through the ECA's convening power, bringing women from around the world together to start to think about how they can push back on this phenomenon. But ultimately we need more proaction.

Mr. POE. Thank you very much.

Chairman?

Chairman ROYCE. Mr. Smith, did you have a follow-up question?

Mr. SMITH. Again, Mr. Watts, I think you wanted to answer the question about a Muslim woman who might defend a non-Muslim woman. Do they use coercive peer pressure against her? Does she become, you know, just like the non-Muslim, raped and abused and exploited?

Mr. WATTS. Well, very simply, she would be subject to the most severe physical punishments. I mean, women receive—Muslim women can receive severe beatings for wearing perfume, for speaking too loudly in public. I met one housewife who, when she had been crossing the street, her big toe slipped out underneath her gown, and she received 50 lashes, she told us, on that big toe for it being revealed. So you can imagine.

I mean, what we did come across was stories where kind of privately and in secret Muslim women from inside ISIS areas had assisted with rescues of non-Muslim women of the Yazidis, either as part of the network or on an individual basis taking extreme risks. But the punishments can be more severe.

Mr. SMITH. And forced conversions, is that a serious problem with the Christians and others?

Mr. WATTS. Yeah. I mean, all the Yazidis, as I think has been mentioned, you know, effectively that was one of the only ways that you could survive in these first few days when a lot of the Yazidis were being captured. There were the mass graves that the chairman mentioned. Men were offered the chance to convert and effectively spare their lives.

Chairman ROYCE. We just want to thank all of our witnesses today. Also, thank you for the time you have put into your prepared testimony.

By the way, that is online. If people want to go to foreignaffairs.house.gov, we will have the Institute for Strategic Dialogue, Sasha, we will have that information and, as a matter of fact, all of your testimony up, if anybody wants to go through your analysis.

And also, I just wanted to say we have several witnesses here who came a continent away to testify before the committee today. Thank you so much. And you have given the committee a lot to think about, and your testimony is going to be very, very valuable to us going forward. So thank you all.

We stand adjourned.

[Whereupon, at 11:55 a.m., the committee was adjourned.]

APPENDIX

MATERIAL SUBMITTED FOR THE RECORD

FULL COMMITTEE HEARING NOTICE
COMMITTEE ON FOREIGN AFFAIRS
U.S. HOUSE OF REPRESENTATIVES
WASHINGTON, DC 20515-6128

Edward R. Royce (R-CA), Chairman

July 29, 2015

TO: MEMBERS OF THE COMMITTEE ON FOREIGN AFFAIRS

You are respectfully requested to attend an OPEN hearing of the Committee on Foreign Affairs, to be held in Room 2172 of the Rayburn House Office Building (and available live on the Committee website at http://www.ForeignAffairs.house.gov):

DATE: Wednesday, July 29, 2015

TIME: 10:00 a.m.

SUBJECT: Women Under ISIS Rule: From Brutality to Recruitment

WITNESSES: Ms. Sasha Havlicek
                 Chief Executive Officer
                 Institute for Strategic Dialogue

                 Ariel Ahram, Ph.D.
                 Assistant Professor
                 Virginia Tech School of Public and International Affairs

                 Mr. Edward Watts
                 Director and Producer
                 Escaping ISIS

                 Kathleen Kuehnast, Ph.D.
                 Director
                 Gender and Peacebuilding
                 Center for Governance, Law and Society
                 United States Institute of Peace

By Direction of the Chairman

COMMITTEE ON FOREIGN AFFAIRS
MINUTES OF FULL COMMITTEE HEARING

Day _Wednesday_ Date _7/29/2015_ Room _2172_

Starting Time _10:06_ Ending Time _11:55_

Recesses _0_ (___ to ___)(___ to ___)(___ to ___)(___ to ___)(___ to ___)(___ to ___)

Presiding Member(s)

Chairman Edward R. Royce

Check all of the following that apply:

Open Session ☑   Electronically Recorded (taped) ☑
Executive (closed) Session ☐   Stenographic Record ☑
Televised ☑

TITLE OF HEARING:

Women Under ISIS: From Brutality to Recruitment

COMMITTEE MEMBERS PRESENT:

See attached.

NON-COMMITTEE MEMBERS PRESENT:

none

HEARING WITNESSES: Same as meeting notice attached? Yes ☑ No ☐
(If "no", please list below and include title, agency, department, or organization.)

STATEMENTS FOR THE RECORD: _(List any statements submitted for the record.)_

SFR - Rep. Ileana Ros-Lehtinen
SFR - Rep. Gerald Connolly
QFR - Chairman Edward R. Royce
QFR - Rep. Ileana Ros-Lehtinen

TIME SCHEDULED TO RECONVENE
or
TIME ADJOURNED _11:55_

Jean Marter, Director of Committee Operations

HOUSE COMMITTEE ON FOREIGN AFFAIRS
FULL COMMITTEE HEARING

PRESENT	MEMBER
X	Edward R. Royce, CA
X	Christopher H. Smith, NJ
X	Ileana Ros-Lehtinen, FL
X	Dana Rohrabacher, CA
X	Steve Chabot, OH
	Joe Wilson, SC
	Michael T. McCaul, TX
X	Ted Poe, TX
X	Matt Salmon, AZ
	Darrell Issa, CA
	Tom Marino, PA
X	Jeff Duncan, SC
	Mo Brooks, AL
	Paul Cook, CA
X	Randy Weber, TX
	Scott Perry, PA
X	Ron DeSantis, FL
	Mark Meadows, NC
X	Ted Yoho, FL
	Curt Clawson, FL
	Scott, DesJarlais, TN
	Reid Ribble, WI
X	Dave Trott, MI
	Lee Zeldin, NY
X	Dan Donovan, NY

PRESENT	MEMBER
X	Eliot L. Engel, NY
X	Brad Sherman, CA
	Gregory W. Meeks, NY
X	Albio Sires, NJ
X	Gerald E. Connolly, VA
	Theodore E. Deutch, FL
	Brian Higgins, NY
	Karen Bass, CA
	William Keating, MA
X	David Cicilline, RI
	Alan Grayson, FL
X	Ami Bera, CA
	Alan S. Lowenthal, CA
X	Grace Meng, NY
X	Lois Frankel, FL
	Tulsi Gabbard, HI
	Joaquin Castro, TX
	Robin Kelly, IL
	Brendan Boyle, PA

Subcommittee Chairman Ros-Lehtinen
Statement
Full Committee Hearing: Women Under ISIL Rule
Wednesday, July 29, 2015

Thank you, Chairman Royce and Ranking Member Engel, for convening this hearing on an important topic that often goes overlooked as we often focus on ISILs spread, its terror and our strategy to combat and defeat the terror group.

Far too often we forget about the victims of ISIL's reign of terror – the religious minorities, the communities that don't adhere to its radical ideology, and the women and children.

But we also fail to address the terror group's sophistication, its increasing manipulation of its sympathizers and its ability to appeal and recruit women from not just the Muslim countries, but from the West as well.

It would seem counterintuitive for a terror group with such a radical interpretation of Islam to allow for a prominent role for women in its organization, especially given the nature of some of the unspeakable crimes against humanity and ISIL carries out against women in the name of Islam against women.

However, for ISIL and other radical Islamic groups, the ends almost always justify means, and using women to achieve their ultimate goal can serve them as an effective tool.

This is such a difficult idea for us to wrap our heads around, because too often we only view women as the victims in this and that leaves us woefully unprepared to address ISIL's manipulation of women as tools for its agenda.

We're already woefully inadequate at countering ISIL's radical ideology and the humanitarian crisis it has caused, but add this into the mix and it becomes readily apparent that our government still lacks both the understanding of the full capabilities of ISIL and a comprehensive approach to counter and defeat the terror group.

Women Under ISIS Rule: From Brutality to Recruitment
CFA Full Committee Hearing
10:00 AM, Wednesday, July 29, 2015
2172 RHOB
Rep. Gerald E. Connolly (D-VA)

This hearing is the first in a series of hearings on the challenges facing women around the globe, and the connection between a nation's security and stability and the status of its women and girls. When half of a country's population is deprived of equal opportunity and protections under the law there is no easy path to national prosperity. This series of hearings is a welcome examination of a serious human rights concern and structural problem that plagues many of the world's volatile regions.

Newspaper headlines have devoted disproportionate attention to the women who have voluntarily travelled to live under the rule of the Islamic State of Iraq and the Levant (ISIL). This is certainly a problem we must understand and combat. However, as is the case elsewhere in the world, the plight of oppressed women under ISIL is not a product of choice. While much attention has been given to the 550 women from Western countries who have emigrated to Syria and Iraq to join ISIL, there are 4 million women and girls living under ISIL, a vast majority of whom are not doing so by choice.

Human rights groups have reported systematic rape, sexual violence, and forced marriages in ISIL-controlled territories. Young women and girls have been separated from their families and forced into a life of servitude. The promise of young brides is used to recruit new fighters for ISIL.

Survivors who have escaped are often in need of psychological support and recovery assistance. Some are survivors of suicide who attempted to take their own lives rather than live in such reprehensible conditions. Many also are afraid to return home for fear that they will bring shame to their families.

The approach to improving the lives of women under ISIL is unique in that the U.S. and its partners are not seeking to reform society under ISIL. Instead, our goal is to degrade and destroy ISIL. So integral is the subjugation of women to ISIL's identity, it is not likely we could divorce the two.

ISIL is not a system to be reformed. It is a state of trauma. Our priorities on behalf of its victims should be to cut off its resources, degrade its capabilities on the battlefield, and help our partners take back the territory over which it so brutally reigns. The humanitarian assistance response to the region should include treatment, education, and training for the severely abused women who have survived ISIL. They deserve to be stakeholders in the region's future.

Questions for the Record from Chairman Ed Royce
For Ms. Sasha Havlicek
"Women Under ISIS Rule: From Brutality to Recruitment" Hearing
July 29, 2015

1. Ms. Havlicek, how do you define "success" when trying to counter violence extremism? Is such "success" possible to measure? If so, how?

While the domain of prevention is notoriously difficult to evaluate, there are both tactical and strategic measures of success in the fight against violent extremism.

At a macro level, the most obvious measures of success are tactical, including a decrease in the annual numbers of terrorist incidents or a decrease in the numbers of foreign fighters and other recruits traveling to join groups like ISIS. While difficult to attribute to any single programme of work, these would be important achievements, though I believe they are not sufficient, in themselves, to define success.

Indeed there was a temporary decrease in terrorist activity linked with Jihadist ideologies between 9/11 and today that belied the underlying fact that the ideology was still being spread more or less unchallenged and was on the rise, as were the identity-based grievances that, in the right geo-political context, could be mobilised very quickly, as we have seen with ISIS.

It is therefore absolutely vital that we define our goals in the CVE space, not only at a tactical level, but also at a strategic level, to address key risk factors. This must include the de-legitimization and undercutting of extremist ideologies, which effectively means achieving a shift in attitudes within the wider circles of tacit support for extremist groups and views. This can be measured through a shift in discourse norms within these networks and environments, which is academically achievable both in the on and offline space, and should be incorporated into the long term evaluation of CVE programming. This is currently not the case.

The key is to incorporate an assessment of levels of non-violent extremism, alongside acts of violent extremism. In reality CVE programmes (both governmental and non-governmental) have, to date, largely been assessed based on what I would call their bureaucratic efficacy (ie. were they well managed and cost effective?). In addition, intervention programmes in many places have focused on pulling individuals back from the edge in terms of their violent intentions, but have often employed non-violent extremists in this process, stopping short of challenging their underlying, justificatory ideology (disengagement, as opposed to deradicalisation). While this might tick the tactical box of preventing an act of terrorism, it may be kicking the problem further down the road, and is failing to address the larger root challenge of draining "the swamp" from which recruiters are able to recruit to violence all too easily. Combining short term tactical measures, with longer term, strategic measures, is vital for success and long term prevention.

On a geostrategic level, I believe tactical alliances with non-ISIS Jihadist groups are equally unwise. While they may result in short term security gains, they are likely to represent a challenge at a later stage, as we have already seen all too often.

At ISD, we take a rigorous metrics based approach to all our intervention work, in particular in the online counter-narrative domain, where we have been working with partners to develop a comprehensive Strategic Intervention, Monitoring and Evaluation Framework. This combines both short and long term indicators of success, based on an in-depth audience segmentation, on the tailored targeting of those groups or individuals, on an evaluation of the nature of the engagement achieved with those audiences and on a longer term analysis of shifts in discourse norms (including levels of support for extremist ideologies) within the wider ecosystems of extremists, on and offline.

2. I understand that as part of you work to counter extremism, your organization facilitates outreach to youth by victims of violent extremism and former extremists themselves. Has there been any research or evidence gathered to date that suggests that outreach by victims and former extremists is an effective way to prevent individuals from becoming radicalized? If so, how does this method compare to other methods of countering violent extremism?

To my knowledge, there have not been any academic studies that involve controlled testing of interventions using formers or survivors, compared to other types of intervention providers. However, convincing and extensive anecdotal evidence can be drawn, not only from our own work with formers at ISD, in particular within the Against Violent Extremism (AVE) network, but from a variety of cases over a long period of time.

In post-war Germany, denazification programming included regular visits to schools by Holocaust survivors. It is well-known that the emotive and personal engagement fostered by such visits was often instrumental in shifting 'hearts and minds'.

Former drug addicts are utilized in school drug programmes as they are often able to engage with young people more effectively than a police officer: their personal experiences give them emotive credibility.

Equally, long standing 'Exit' programmes established in countries such as Sweden and Germany to address Far Right and neo-Nazi radicalization have tended to be run by formers or have used formers as intervention providers. These programmes have now started to be replicated in other countries as a result of their successes.

Finally, ISD has just released a report last week on a pioneering programme of One-to-One Online Interventions which has facilitated direct online contact between former extremists (Islamists in the UK and Far Right in the US) and individuals identified on Facebook by the project as being 'at risk' of radicalization and recruitment. The results from this relatively small piece of action research have been surprising, in that a 60% sustained engagement was achieved, coded as five or more messages being exchanged and a meaningful conversation entered into between the candidate and the intervention provider. While engagement does not constitute success in itself, it is an extremely important step in the process of deradicalisation or counter-radicalisation, and from the perspective both of identifying risk as well as redressing risk, this programme is possibly the first to substantiate the instrumental role that formers can play.

Subcommittee Chairman Ros-Lehtinen
Questions
Full Committee Hearing: Women Under ISIL Rule
Wednesday, July 29, 2015

1. Ms. Havlicek, we often say that education is this great equalizer, that societies that allow access to education for girls and women promote a more inclusive and productive society, and that it's no coincidence that the countries most susceptible to human trafficking, exploitation and radicalization are those that restrict a woman's access to education. As you note, however, there is an increasing amount of young girls and women being lured to ISIL from the West, where presumably they had access to education.
   What is it about the lure of ISIL that is so strong that can attract these educated girls and women to leave their homes and join the cause, how difficult does that make our efforts to counter ISIL, and how do we address this problem?

It is true that we are seeing young women (and men) being radicalized and recruited to ISIS from a variety of socio-economic and educational backgrounds. The girls and women being recruited from Western Countries are also more educated than their male counterparts. While educated mothers, as the primary vectors of social and cultural transmission, have a better chance of staving off reactionary and extremist tendencies in their children, many of the young people we see radicalizing are rebelling against the (often conservative) norms of their parents' generation, in favour of the militancy of extremist doctrines.

While there is no question that societies benefit as a whole from higher levels of female educational attainment, the causes of radicalization among women, as among men, are multifold. Questions relating to identity, in particular Muslim identity, within a Western environment characterized by rising anti-Muslim sentiment and discrimination; frustration and anger regarding the suffering of Muslim communities worldwide and the real or perceived inaction of Western governments in response; the notion that Western concepts of feminism have ultimately objectified and demeaned women; these are all very present in the discourse of those girls and women that have joined ISIS that we have been tracking with our research.

These emotive issues, which are exploited very successfully by the extremist propaganda machinery, appeal across a wide cross section of people. Indeed higher levels of political and social awareness may contribute to an interest in, and engagement with, what has increasingly become the counter-culture of our time.

It is also important to note that the girls and women that have joined ISIS from the West, whose online lives we have been monitoring, are clearly ideologically committed to the Jihadist cause and as such, submit willingly to its strictures relating to women. It is often assumed that women are less likely to be ideologically radicalized and committed. That is of course not the case.

Our response must therefore be to look at the causes of this radicalization process both in terms of push factors (which I would define less in purely socio-economic terms and more in terms of questions of identity that need to be addressed) as well as pull factors (global efforts to propagate the ideologies that constitute the intellectual foundations of groups like ISIS). In my written testimony, I refer to a number of ways in which I believe this ideological challenge might be addressed.

2. For the panel: In many parts of the region, women are second class citizens with few rights and subject to their husbands or the men in their family – so how can we begin to effectively address sexual violence without first or simultaneously addressing the issue of a more inclusive society that accepts gender equality?

Havlicek: I believe we must continue actively to encourage and support the Human Rights of women globally. We know that this can be done most effectively through painstaking work at grassroots levels, working with communities on a long-term basis, engaging all relevant stakeholders in order to shift norms where needed. Long-term investments must be made as a matter of strategic importance. There has been a marked dip in appetite for support to Human Rights work internationally over the last decade. This needs to be redressed.

Ahram: Thank you Congresswoman Ros-Lehtinen for your question. You are exactly right concerning the broader issue of the treatment of women in Arab society. The Arab Human Development Report, a report written by some of the prominent Arab intellectuals working under the sponsorship of the United Nations Development Program, has found persistent patterns of women's political and social exclusion. This has had profoundly negative consequences for political reform and economic development in the Arab world as a whole. ISIS's use of sexual violence unfortunately reflects many social and political practices common in the Arab world.

However, when it comes to the particular situation of women and children in Syria and Iraq, it is important to note the deleterious impact of war. In the 1950s until the 1980s, Syria and Iraq were among the most progressive Arab countries when it came to women's rights. At least some of this improvement came about because authoritarian rulers sought to weaken the power of clergy and other conservative social elements by promoting women's rights to education and jobs and equality in the law. For the first time in history women in both countries joined the labor force on a large scale, gained broad access to higher education, and had significant rights to divorce and inheritance. In Iraq, nearly three decades of continual war, beginning with the Iran-Iraq war in 1980 and running through the Gulf War in 1991, the American invasion of 2003 and the civil war of 2003 to 2008, has caused a drastic degradation in women's status. In Syria, the brutality of the civil war has had a similar effect since 2011.

Much of the harm to women comes through population displacement. As the United Nations Refugee Agency has shown repeatedly, women and children that become refugees or internally displaced peoples (IDPs) are the most susceptible to sexual exploitation, including human trafficking. They are often in desperate financial straits, have no access to education or employment, and have lost larger family connections necessary for protection and support. In Syria nearly forty percent of the population, at 10 million people have, have become refugees or IDPs. In Iraq, there are about four million refugees and IDPs. Direct intervention to help women and children in these conditions is an emergency that must be addressed before even considering a broader agenda for societal change.